SKYBREAK

THE 58TH FIGHTER SQUADRON
—— IN DESERT STORM ——

MIKE GUARDIA

From *Debrief: A Complete History of US Aerial Engagements, 1981-present* by Craig Brown. Used by permission of Schiffer Publishing. Any third-party use of this material, outside of this publication, is prohibited. Interested parties must apply directly to Schiffer Publishing for permission.

From *Call-Sign Kluso: An American Fighter Pilot in Mr. Reagan's Air Force* by Rick Tollini. Used by permission of Casemate Publishers. Any third-party use of this material, outside of this publication, is prohibited. Interested parties must apply directly to Casemate Publishers for permission.

From *Separated by War: An Oral History by Desert Storm Fliers and Their Families* by Ed Herlik. Used by permission of Ed Herlik. Any third-party use of this material, outside of this publication, is prohibited. Interested parties must apply directly to Ed Herlik for permission.

Published by Magnum Books
PO Box 1661
Maple Grove, MN 55311

www.mikeguardia.com

ISBN-13: 978-0-9996443-7-9

For Marie and Melanie...

And dedicated to the memory of Chief Master Sergeant Jose Matos (1948-2021), who tragically passed away while this book was in production.

Contents

INTRODUCTION

In the summer of 1990, mankind stood on the brink of a new era. Gone were the days of the Cold War—the Iron Curtain had fallen, Germany had reunified, and the once-mighty Soviet Union lay on its deathbed. But as Communism faded from Eastern Europe, and America reaped the benefits of her new "peace dividend," a new conflict loomed on the horizon.

On the morning of August 2, 1990, Iraqi forces under the command of Saddam Hussein invaded the tiny emirate of Kuwait. Within hours, the Kuwaiti defenses collapsed under the onslaught of the Iraqi Army. The invasion drew fierce condemnation from the international community and prompted the United Nations to demand Saddam's withdrawal. Undeterred by the rhetoric, the Iraqi dictator massed his forces along the Saudi Arabian border and dared the world to stop him. In response, the US military led a coalition of thirty-four nations in what became Operation Desert Storm—a violent air and ground campaign to eject the Iraqis from Kuwait.

At the tip of the spear were the men of the US Air Force's 58th Fighter Squadron. Mounted aboard their F-15C Eagle fighter jets, these young aviators took to the sky against the

Iraqi Air Force, a battle-hardened cadre of fighter pilots with recent combat experience from the Iran-Iraq War. Although confident in their capabilities, and the quality of their F-15s, these untested American pilots were flying into combat against the "latest and greatest" aircraft from the latter-day Soviet Union—including the MiG-29 and Sukhoi Su-24.

However, despite the odds, and their lack of combat experience, the 58th Fighter Squadron decimated the Iraqi Air Force in one engagement after another. On the first day of the air war—January 17, 1991—Captain Jon "JB" Kelk claimed the first aerial victory of Desert Storm, downing the first MiG-29 in combat. In less than 30 days, the 58th Fighter Squadron flew more than 1,600 combat sorties and destroyed 16 Iraqi aircraft—more than any other coalition unit. Indeed, over the course of Desert Storm, the 58th Fighter Squadron accomplished feats that no other air unit matched. These included: the most air-to-air kills; the most double kills; the most sorties and hours flown by an F-15 unit in theater; and the highest number of MiG-29s destroyed by a single unit (five in total).

Stationed at Eglin Air Force Base, Florida, the 58th Fighter Squadron was America's premier F-15 unit. Activated in 1941, the 58th Fighter Squadron served with distinction in both the Mediterranean and China-Burma-India Theaters of World War II. During operations in the Mediterranean Theater, the squadron earned its nickname "The Gorillas" for their unorthodox, guerrilla-style flying techniques. Throughout its various campaigns over Europe and Asia, the 58th flew iconic aircraft such as the P-40 Warhawk, P-47 Thunderbolt, and P-38 Lightning. In 1950, the squadron was among the first to receive the new F-86 Sabre, followed soon thereafter by the F-89D Scorpion. By the early 1970s, the 58th Fighter Squadron had received the ubiquitous F-4 Phantom II—the iconic fighter jet of the Vietnam era. In 1972, the squadron deployed to Udorn

Royal Thai Air Force Base, flying combat missions over Vietnam. During this deployment, the 58th scored two air-to-air victories against North Vietnamese aircraft—downing a MiG-19 and MiG-21. In 1979, the 58th became the first squadron in the 33d Fighter Wing to receive the new F-15 Eagle. The F-15 would remain the squadron's primary aircraft until September 2009, when the 58th became the first F-35 Lighting II "Joint Strike Fighter" training unit.

The idea for *Skybreak* began in the Fall of 2019 as I finished my previous book, *Wings of Fire: A Combat History of the F-15*. Throughout my research, I was astounded by the accomplishments of American F-15 pilots and their ground crews during Desert Storm. Although the F-15 had seen combat with the Israeli Air Force in the skies over Lebanon, it remained untested in the hands of American pilots. The Iraqi Air Force, meanwhile, was the largest in the Middle East and they had recent combat experience from their eight-year war with Iran. Yet, in spite of the odds, American pilots handily defeated the Iraqi Air Force in a matter of weeks. Throughout the conflict, several fighter squadrons earned distinction for their air-to-air engagements. None, however, matched the accomplishments of the 58th Fighter Squadron. Aside from their record-setting kill ratios, the squadron's maintenance crews worked tirelessly to keep their F-15s aloft. Their efforts kept the squadron at an astonishing 98% readiness rate—a feat that was unheard of even during peacetime. I was also surprised that, despite their accomplishments during Desert Storm, no one had yet written a book about the 58th Fighter Squadron.

The Gulf War remains one of the most defining events of the latter 20th Century. The origins and outcomes of Desert Storm still resonate within the political discourse of the Middle East. Moreover, America's victory in that conflict underscored the remarkable transformation that its military had undergone during the post-Vietnam era. It was also the first war fought predominantly by a generation of post-Baby Boomers. Indeed, the elder members of Generation X (born between 1964-72) did most of the fighting and dying on the frontlines in Iraq. For the elder Millennials like myself (born after 1980), Desert Storm was the first major conflict that occurred during our lifetime. We were in grade school at the time, but many of us remember watching the nightly news with our parents, listening to the likes of Peter Jennings and Ted Koppel as they narrated the events unfolding halfway around the world. Some of our parents were mobilized reservists and, in our classrooms and churches, we drew pictures of the American flag and sponsored care packages for those serving in the Gulf. The Desert Camouflage pattern became a fashion statement for kids nationwide and "Stormin Norman" became a household name.

Several pilots and maintenance crewmen graciously gave their time for interviews—sharing memories and photographs from their time in the 58th Fighter Squadron. Their interviews and photographic keepsakes have formed the backbone of this narrative. The reader must bear in mind, however, that time and monetary constraints prevented me from interviewing *every* pilot in the squadron. Some never responded to the inquiry; some politely declined to be interviewed; others have tragically passed on; while others simply couldn't be found. My search to locate these missing airmen returned only a handful of dead phone numbers or addresses that had long since changed.

The reader must also bear in mind that this is a book about the 58th Fighter Squadron. Their experiences are the driving force behind the narrative. Therefore, the reader will not find many detailed discussions about the broader aspects of the Gulf War. While I have included *some* discussion of these aspects for the sake of context, they are discussed largely inasmuch as they relate to the 58th's deployment. My intent is to provide the reader with an intimate, no-holds-barred account of modern air-to-air combat, as told by the brave men who lived it.

Skybreak is their story.

Chapter 1
THE VANGUARDS

RICK "KLUSO" TOLLINI

Contrary to what Hollywood portrays, a fighter pilot's callsign is rarely glamorous or inspiring. Indeed, the exotic and tough-sounding callsigns like "Maverick" and "Iceman," are the province of Hollywood fiction. "The act of receiving a tactical callsign," said Rick Tollini, "is a very historical and sometimes complex process. Usually, callsigns are based

Rick "Kluso" Tollini.

on something that makes you 'famous'—like gross stupidity during training; or 'natural' callsigns that go with your name—like 'Dusty' Rhoades, 'Notso' Biggs; or based on the way you look. For me, it was that many people thought I looked like Inspector Clouseau from *The Pink Panther.*" Thus, when spelled in colloquial fighter pilot phonetics, Tollini was given the callsign "Kluso."

A pilot almost never got to choose his own callsign. It was typically given to him by his classmates at the conclusion of his flight training, or given by his chain-of-command upon arriving at his first squadron. Those who were included in the callsign selection process sometimes strove to create a callsign that the pilot hated. Reflecting on "Kluso," Tollini remarked: "It could have been worse."

Rick Tollini was the Weapons Officer for the 58th Fighter Squadron—a designation that made him responsible for the unit's combat preparations. Yet his path to the military was an unlikely one. Born and raised in Stockton, California, Tollini was the product of what he called a "typical Baby Boomer suburb." He was the youngest of three children born to a middle-class family whose mother was an elementary teacher and whose patriarch was a civil aircraft mechanic. The elder Tollini was also a private pilot. Thus, it came as little surprise that his aeronautical career sparked his son's interest in flight.

Accompanying his father on many local flights, Rick developed a near-insatiable appetite for military aviation history. "I was fascinated by the men, machines, and war stories." Every year, his family attended the annual Reno Air Races, where a young Tollini saw vintage warbirds take flight in aerial maneuvers across the Nevada sky.

Surprisingly, however, Rick admitted that: "I had absolutely no desire to enter the military. My intent from high school all the way through college was to work/fly my way into the civilian airlines." To that end, Rick Tollini enrolled in the Aeronautics Department at San Jose State University (SJSU). The Aeronautics Department, as he recalled, was a trade program similar in scope to the courses offered at the renowned Embry-Riddle Aeronautical University, where students completed degree requirements towards a commercial aircraft license. During this time, Tollini described himself as the quintessential "California hippie," complete with long hair and a beard to match. "I was too young to be part of the late-60s generation, but this was the typical California persona back then—long hair, bell bottoms and the like," he said with a chuckle.

After completing his aircraft license, Rick worked as a civil flight instructor. It was a necessary step in the early years of a commercial pilot; all the major and regional airlines required a certain number of flight hours before considering candidates for hire. Most applicants satisfied these requirements via flight instruction or prior service as a military pilot.

While serving as a flight instructor, Tollini also taught ground-based classes at SJSU. At around this time, however, Rick began to consider the Air Force as a viable career. It was the dawn of the 1980s and America's military was beginning to lift itself from the post-Vietnam malaise. In the dying days of the Carter Administration, military spending became a top priority. Ronald Reagan carried the momentum forward, and all branches of the military began re-branding themselves as elite, high-tech, all-volunteer outfits dedicated to defending freedom.

Walking into the local recruiting station, Rick calmly asked: "What do I need to do to join the Air Force?" The recruiter, taking pause just long enough to study Tollini's long hair and beard, heartily guffawed. "Yeah, right!" chuckled the recruiter. Pleading his case, however, Rick got the recruiter's attention when he said he was a licensed pilot with a degree in aeronautical technology.

"Well," said the recruiter, "let's get the paperwork ready."

His decision to join the military was "abrupt," as he recalled –"and a 180-degree flip from where I was going"— but it was a move that would precipitate a 20+ year career as a distinguished pilot.

Based on his education, Rick qualified for both officer and pilot training. In the summer of 1982, he reported to Officer Training School (OTS) at Lackland Air Force Base in San Antonio, Texas. A rigorous 90-day training course, OTS prepared civilians for the mental and physical rigors of Air Force officership. Upon graduation, officer trainees would receive commissions as second lieutenants and begin specialty training in their desired career field. For the young Rick Tollini, OTS was a proverbial "culture shock." The whirlwind intensity of the course, and the constant furor of the Military Training Instructors (MTIs—ie Air Force Drill Sergeants) left him exhausted at the end of every day.

Yet, with every passing week, Tollini gained more admiration for the Air Force and its personnel. During his formative years in California, particularly during the 1970s, Tollini recalled that there was still an air of anti-war sentiment left over from Vietnam. "I actually had a draft lottery number, but fortunately the draft ended before I could get called up." Prior to joining the Air Force, Tollini admitted that the military was "totally foreign and unfamiliar" to him. "I always thought that maybe people go into the military voluntarily because they didn't have any other choices. But that changed...I soon realized that the Air Force was abundant with high-level professionals...and it was not the way it had been portrayed in the books/movies of the previous decade. By the time I finished OTS, I felt like I was in the best possible place I could be, and the idea of service to country was something I wanted to embrace."

He credited President Ronald Reagan with revitalizing America's military and "turning around America's shame or regret" over the war in Vietnam. In fact, it was the Reagan buildup that had allowed Tollini to become a pilot. "The Air Force was in a huge buildup of tactical aviation at the time," he said, "and they were aggressively recruiting people like me, fresh out of college...with flying experience."

Still, navigating OTS was no simple matter.

"A lot of guys dropped out," he recalled. "Even guys with pilot slots."

But he found that as long as he took one day at a time, he could easily conquer the beast of OTS.

Graduating from Lackland that fall, Tollini sensed a renewed vigor amongst his fellow airmen. "It seemed like everyone was fired up.," he said, "from all us young aviators, to the senior officers who had made it through the rough years of downsizing. It was like something big was waiting for us."

How right he was.

Due to his extensive flight experience, Tollini had joined the Air Force with a guaranteed pilot contract. Before earning his wings, however, he would have to endure a seemingly endless battery of medical exams—administered by some of the most renowned flight surgeons in the country. "The biggest worry," he said, "was that they would find something that would physically disqualify you from pilot training." Although the Air Force desperately needed pilots, they were unyielding in their medical standards. Those who passed the rigid flight physicals were sent along to Undergraduate Pilot Training (UPT). "By the way," he added, "the age limit to enter UPT was 27; I squeaked in at 26-and-a-half!"

Because Tollini already had a private pilot's license, his

UPT at Williams Air Force Base was essentially a review session. "For those who did not have *any* flight experience, they had to go to a very basic flight course, flying T-41s [military-grade Cessna 172s] to get them to a basic solo capability." For those who possessed at least twenty hours of flight time, or a civilian pilot rating (like Tollini), they would begin UPT aboard the T-37 jet trainer.

The T-37 module began with basic jet-operating skills— "takeoff, navigation patterns, landing...and eventually progressed to basic aerobatics. Most of us who had previous flight experience pretty much breezed through this course."

Still, Tollini recalled that this module of UPT had a high dropout rate.

"Sometimes it was the inability to overcome air sickness, or a recognition that somebody didn't have the skills or couldn't keep up with the pace of the course." Most, however, passed the T-37 module and progressed to the T-38 module. "The T-38 was fun to fly, but also very challenging. None of us had flown anything that fast, and it wasn't really easy to land. The T-38 was designed to train Century-series [F-100 series] pilots. Those jets had a critical flight envelope."

Whether aboard the T-37 or T-38, the flight trainees were constantly challenged and evaluated by their instructors. "Before the end of UPT," said Rick, "there is a consolidated consensus among the instructor pilots about who will be designated fighter-qualified...usually the top 30%." Those who were designated fighter-qualified were eligible to fly fighters (F-4s, F-15s, and F-16s) or attack aircraft (A-10s, F-111s, etc). Those beyond the top 30% were typically assigned to heavy bombers or other crew-manned aircraft such as troop carriers or aero-tankers. At the end of UPT, Rick was elated to discover that his class rank qualified him for a fighter assignment.

To this point, his only aspiration had been to fly the F-111 Aardvark. Despite its fighter designation "F" prefix, the F-111 was actually an attack aircraft. Tollini had been fascinated by the F-111 since its tumultuous debut as an abortive carrier-based fighter. However, when he discovered that the F-111 squadrons were assigned to the least desirable Air Force bases, he quickly changed his mind, opting for the F-15 Eagle.

Reporting to Fighter Lead-In Training (FLIT) at Holloman Air Force, New Mexico, Tollini described it as "another T-38 program but with more emphasis on maximum performance maneuvers, basic fighter tactics, and advanced combat maneuvers." These included dogfighting maneuvers for "one-on-one" and "two-on-one" scenarios. FLIT was then proceeded by the F-15 Familiarization Course at Luke Air Force Base, Arizona. "Learning to fly the Eagle was easy—takeoffs, landings, formations—it's a very easy airplane to fly hands-on." Learning to operate the complex weapons systems, however—and use them in a high-speed dogfight—was much more difficult. Still, flying the F-15 was a tremendous experience for the young Rick Tollini. The plane was, by every measure, the most-advanced fighter jet in the world. Although it had yet to see combat in American service, the F-15 had proven its might in the Israeli Air Force during the latter-day air wars against Syrian MiGs over Lebanon. If that conflict was any indication, the F-15 was certain to be the king of air superiority for at least another generation.

Tollini's first assignment as a newly-minted "Eagle Driver" was to the 12th Fighter Squadron, "The Dirty Dozen," at Kadena Air Base in Okinawa. "The Dirty Dozen," he said, "had a special culture of high standards and excellence. To me, they stood out over every other squadron on the base… and that culture perpetuated itself generation after generation, even with people and leaders coming and going. I credit my experience in the Dirty Dozen for everything else that followed. It was the best place to learn to be an Eagle driver." Given its strategic location on Okinawa (i.e. close proximity to China, North Korea, and the eastern outposts of the Soviet Union), the 12th Fighter Squadron had the best opportunities for training deployments—particularly among the Pacific Rim partners. "I left Kadena as a fully-qualified instructor pilot and flight examiner," two ratings that would help him immensely when he was reassigned to the 58th Fighter Squadron in the fall of 1987.

His reassignment to the 58th had been at the behest of Lieutenant Colonel Frank "Paco" Geisler, the squadron commander. Geisler was already a legend in the fighter community. With a distinguished combat record in Vietnam, Geisler had also flown with the "Red Eagles"—America's clandestine MiG squadron. Flying "secretly acquired" MiG aircraft, the Red Eagles served as mock aggressors in various training exercises to prepare other American pilots for dogfights against Soviet and Eastern Bloc aircraft. Geisler had assumed command of the 58th shortly before the squadron received its newest iteration of the F-15C Eagle: the so-called "Multi-Stage Improvement Program (MSIP) Eagles." These MSIP variants had upgraded engines and improved avionics/weapons systems.

"For that reason," said Tollini, "Paco was able to hand-pick some of the most experienced F-15 pilots coming to Eglin"—which included Rick Tollini and several others who would later deploy to the Persian Gulf. "Eventually," he said, "I was selected to attend the USAF Fighter Weapons School,"—the Air Force equivalent to the Navy's "TOPGUN" program. Tollini graduated at the top of his class in December 1989, earning the coveted title of "Weapons Officer." When he returned to the 58th as the Squadron Weapons Officer, his duties took on a whole new dimension. As a subject-matter expert on fighter weapons, tactics, and engagement, it was Tollini's job to train the squadron for combat. "Having that opportunity, and actually taking your squadron to war, is what every weapons officer desires…and that was my position when we deployed to Desert Storm."

Cesar "Rico" Rodriguez

Perhaps it was inevitable that Cesar Rodriguez would land the callsign "Rico." He was a gifted pilot and had done nothing to warrant a punitive callsign; and his name didn't necessarily lend itself to any creative monikers, so geography would ultimately determine his lifelong callsign. As a young pilot stationed in Korea, Rodriguez and his friends frequented a local bar/restaurant outside the Suwon Air Base. The proprietor, a middle-aged woman who had been serving American GIs for decades, asked Rodriguez and his comrades (who, by now, were regular customers) for their first names.

Cesar "Rico" Rodriguez and his Crew Chief.

He told her his first name was "Cesar," but due to her native Korean phonetics, she had trouble pronouncing it. "So she asked me:'Where are you from?'And I told her my last home was Puerto Rico."

"Ok," she replied. "I'm going to call you Rico!"

The name stuck, and it eventually became his callsign.

Born in El Paso, Texas in 1959, Cesar Rodriguez was the son of a US Army officer. Living the life of a quintessential Army brat, Rodriguez grew up among several different Army posts—including Fort Bliss, Aberdeen Proving Grounds, and even Panama. During the days of the Panama Canal Zone, the US Army manned several garrisons along the territorial stretch of the Panama Canal. Rodriguez recalled that the trip to Panama was an adventure unto itself.

Indeed, the family made the journey *by car.*

Along the famous Inter-American Highway, the elder Rodriguez piled his family into their car for the 1,500-mile trip through Mexico, Guatemala, Nicaragua, and the various banana republics before reaching the entry point to the Canal Zone. The younger Rodriguez described his father as a "tough love" kind of guy, but one who nevertheless instilled in his children a solid work ethic, a sense of fair play, and a love of sports. Indeed, like many military kids in 20th Century America, Cesar immersed himself in the local variety of team sports wherever his family was stationed. While attending the School of the Americas in Panama, Rodriguez was a starting quarterback for the varsity football team and earned his Eagle Scout badge by his sophomore year.

When his father received orders to Fort Buchanan, Puerto Rico, the young Rodriguez began weighing his options for college. "My football coach [in Puerto Rico] had been a line coach at West Point for a while," he said, and thus encouraged Rodriguez to send tapes of his highlighted football games to the athletic departments at West Point and other military colleges. "I was pretty confident that I wanted to be an officer," said Rodriguez, "and I was thinking I'd go the Army route."

But West Point accepted him only on the provision that he first attend the Academy's prep school at Fort Monmouth, New Jersey for one year prior to admission. "I wasn't interested in doing a five-year program [one year at the prep school, followed by four years at West Point], so I sent my tapes to VMI and the Citadel"—the latter of which offered him a partial scholarship for football and baseball. "And that's how I started my college career: thinking I was going to be an Army officer."

Halfway through his sophomore year, however, Rodriguez and his roommate sat for an inter-service aviation test battery. "All the services were testing for their flight schools," he said, and Citadel cadets had the opportunity to sit for each exam as part of a day-long testing cycle. "The first test was the Army Aviation Aptitude Test. Then we took the Navy test; then the Air Force test; and then we did the Marine Corps'. It was like two and a half hours for each test." When the test results were published, he discovered that he was one of only seven cadets in his testing group to qualify for Air Force flight training. He had also qualified for the Army and Navy flight programs, but the Air Force offered him the best benefits—including a full scholarship for his last two years at the Citadel."

Graduating from the Citadel in 1981, Cesar Rodriguez commissioned into an Air Force that was reemerging from the bitterness of the post-Vietnam era. Slowly but surely, the aging F-4 Phantom was yielding the flight line to newer, more agile aircraft like the F-15 Eagle and F-16 Fighting Falcon. Meanwhile the USAF expanded its force structure to include forty fighter wings and created new squadrons to accommodate the burgeoning missions of Electronic Warfare (EW) and Suppression of Enemy Air Defenses (SEAD).

Reporting to UPT at Vance Air Force Base in Enid, Oklahoma, Rodriguez began his journey aboard the T-37 and T-38 jet trainers—both of which were admittedly difficult to master. "The physical part of flying was easy," he said, "but the whole concept of instrument cross-checks [and mastering the onboard avionics] was really hard." But, true to his upbringing, Rodriguez persevered and sought after-hours instruction to master the areas in which he struggled.

His perseverance paid off.

By the time he graduated from the T-38 portion of UPT, he was ranked #2 in his class. His class rank qualified him for any category of flight duty within the Air Force.

Ironically, Rodriguez began his career not as a fighter pilot, but as an attack pilot, flying A-10 Thunderbolts (more commonly known as the "Warthog"). His first duty station as an A-10 pilot was Suwon Air Base in Korea, where he served from March 1983 until May 1985. Returning stateside to Holloman Air Force Base, Rodriguez decided to make the transition from attack pilot to fighter pilot. Passing the F-15 familiarization course, Rodriguez found the plane to be nimble, resilient, and quite user-friendly. By the mid-1980s, the F-15 Eagle had emerged as the crown jewel of America's fighter squadrons. Although American F-15s had yet to fire a shot in anger, Israeli F-15s had dominated the skies over the Middle East. Their Arab opponents, meanwhile, had been piloting latter-day Soviet airframes like the MiG-23 and MiG-25. The geopolitical irony was apparent. Indeed, the much-anticipated showdown between American and Soviet-built fighters was happening not in the skies over Europe, but in the Middle East.

As a newly-minted "Eagle driver," Rodriguez found himself assigned to the 58th Fighter Squadron. Almost instantly, he could tell that the 58th was a different kind of unit. "They had a strong reputation and high standards."

When Rodriguez arrived at the squadron in early 1988, "Paco" Geisler was still the squadron commander. Under the latter's guidance, Rodriguez recalled, the 58th Fighter Squadron was on the "leading edge of F-15 tactics and weapons systems." Indeed, many of the senior leaders at Eglin Air Force Base were graduates of the Fighter Weapons School or had flown combat missions in Vietnam. With Geisler at the helm, the 58th essentially had "first right of refusal" for any priority training missions. In fact, any time the Air Force needed an F-15 squadron for special training or developmental exercises, Paco Geisler would get the call.

"Hey, can you bring six jets down here for six weeks?"

And within days, a flight of F-15s from Eglin would be en route to the site of the training mission. "Paco really set the tone for the success of the 58th Fighter Squadron in peacetime and in combat," said Rodriguez. The emphasis on training and standards would pay enormous dividends when they received the order to deploy to Saudi Arabia.

Jon "JB" Kelk

Born and raised in Eau Claire, Wisconsin, Jon Kelk grew up with a deep-seated interest in all things aviation. "I had been interested in flying, really, since I was a young lad." One of his earliest childhood memories was watching the North Central Airlines' Convair CV-580s touching down at the regional airport. Feeding his appetite for aviation, Kelk spent his formative years devouring as many books on the subject as he could find. Although his family had no military lineage per se, the young Kelk took a strong liking to military aviation. "I read books on bombers, fighters, all that stuff...I knew my planes," he chuckled.

But his love of aviation was no passing fancy. "I started flying when I was in high school," he said. "My first job was

Jon "JB" Kelk (pictured here as a Major General in 2016).

as a janitor in a body shop; I took that money and poured it into flying lessons." Indeed, by the time he was 17, he had earned his private pilot license. After graduating from high school, and while attending the University of Wisconsin (UW)—Eau Claire, Jon took a part-time job at the local airport as a "line boy." As he described it, line boys worked the flight line, fueling planes and performing low-level maintenance. His job at the airport also allowed him a discounted rate to pursue his aircraft instrument rating and earn a flight instructor certification. "So, by the time I finished college, I had been a flight instructor for nearly two years."

Graduating from UW-Eau Claire in 1980, Jon had intended to become a civilian pilot—either for the airlines or a commercial freighter. But, as he admitted: "in the late 70s and early 80s, general aviation wasn't doing too well." Indeed, the energy crisis and lingering "stagflation" had taken their toll on the aviation industry. Determined to wait out the hiring slump, Kelk decided to put his accounting degree to good use. While interviewing for accounting jobs, Kelk had been reading the *Wall Street Journal* to stay abreast of happenings in the business world. One day, however, when opening the front page of his latest edition, he saw a headline reading: "Air Force Short 2,000 Pilots."

"Oh really?" he told himself. "Is that so?"

He took the article to the local Air Force recruiter and, "three months later, I had short hair and was learning how to salute." Reporting to OTS at Lackland Air Force Base, Kelk recalled the experience as a true culture shock, but a "means to an end." As he described it, most of the officer candidates were thinking: "All right, let's get through this so we can go off to pilot training."

Like many of his comrades, Kelk noticed that the Air Force was slowly lifting itself from the post-Vietnam malaise. "It was really a turning point," he said. "If you think about the end of the Vietnam War…the Iran crisis, the failed rescue attempt…it wasn't a good time for the country. Thank goodness we beat the Russians in hockey, though!" But Kelk noted that, during his first few years in the military, "things changed dramatically in terms of defense spending. Reagan came in and opened the spigot. And just like any organization, if you're there during a time of increased spending, it's going to be a fun time."

At OTS, he realized just how fortunate he had been to join the Air Force on the cusp of the Reagan buildup. "It took me three months from when I first met the recruiter to get all my things done and report to OTS." However, many of his OTS and flight school comrades had been waiting for *years* to attend. They had submitted their applications during the Ford-Carter years, and had become part of an increasing backlog of applicants who couldn't be processed because the post-Vietnam defense budgets wouldn't allow it.

UPT was relatively easy for the young Kelk, given his extensive background in civil aviation. But he still had to learn the "Air Force way of flying"—which included complex maneuvers and flying in formation. Still, he mastered the T-37 and T-38 with enough skill to earn an endorsement for "Fighter/Attack/Recon" (FAR) training. He was happy to earn the FAR designation, but he initially had other plans. "I thought I would eventually get back to the civilian world," he said. "And in the early 80s, the conventional wisdom was that if you were going to get hired by an airline, you needed to be hired by the time you were 30 or you'd be considered too old." By his calculation, his six-year commitment to the Air Force would allow him to leave by age 28—well within tolerance of the airlines' purported hiring standards. With this in mind, Kelk strongly considered volunteering for duty on an aircraft that would make him more marketable to a prospective airline. He thus considered piloting a C-141 or another large transport comparable to the 707s or Airbuses that flew the friendly skies.

He changed his mind, however, when during UPT, the Air Force brought in a variety of fighter and attack aircraft for the students' familiarization. Kelk recalled that the demonstrators included the F-15, F-16, A-10, and F-111. "I just remember seeing the F-15 and saying: 'That is beautiful.'" Moreover, he convinced himself that if he had the opportunity to fly fighters, he shouldn't pass it up. The so-called "Fighter Pilot Mafia" ran deep within the Air Force culture; many of its senior leaders and influencers had come from the fighter community. An F-15 pilot could presumably write his own ticket for any post-career aviation job. "So, I put F-15 as my first choice."

His first assignment as a newly-minted F-15 driver was to the 8th Fighter Squadron, "The Black Sheep," at Holloman Air Force Base. It was with the Black Sheep that Kelk earned his callsign "JB." At the time, he looked much younger than his 22 years suggested. "Here I was this young, skinny, blonde-haired kid flying fighters"—which earned him the callsign "Jon Boy." Over the years, his wingmen eventually shortened it to "JB."

Every fighter pilot remembers his first unit as his "indoctrination" into the culture of the operational Air Force—away from the academic confines and dogmatic regimentation of OTS and UPT. "It was a blast," he said. "Every day I learned something new." He was deeply impressed by the senior leaders in the squadron, some of whom were certified "MiG killers"—men who had shot down North Vietnamese MiGs over Southeast Asia.

During his time with the Black Sheep squadron, Kelk deployed to West Germany for one of many annual training missions that the Air Force conducted along the Iron Curtain. The Cold War was still at the forefront of American defense policy and the USAF flew various training missions in the skies over Western Europe. During these training sorties, NATO pilots would often catch a glimpse of a MiG-25 or MiG-29, piloted by forward-stationed units of the Soviet Air Force or the East German *Luftstreitkräfte*.

Flying their sorties from Bitburg Air Base in West Germany, Kelk was so enthralled by the base itself and the high-tempo opportunities that, upon his return to Holloman, he requested a transfer to Bitburg as soon as an opening came available. He told his squadron commander:

"I don't care what it takes, but *please* get me to Bitburg, Germany."

Two months later, his squadron commander came to him and said:

"Hey, I don't know if you've heard this, but Bitburg is sending a guy home."

Apparently, that pilot's wife was having trouble adapting to life in West Germany. Thus, Bitburg's command group was sending him back to the States, and Bitburg wanted a stateside pilot to take his place. Having spent more than a year and a half with the Black Sheep at Holloman, Kelk was eligible for a transfer if he still wanted it. A few days later, he was en route to Bitburg as an incoming member of the 525th Fighter Squadron, "Bulldogs."

It was now the summer of 1984, and JB Kelk would spend the next four years of his career flying missions along the Iron Curtain. Because the defense of Western Europe was a top priority for America's military, his assignment to the 525th meant "lots of flying hours and lots of deployments...it just couldn't have been any better." By the summer of 1988, though, his tour in Germany was coming to a close and the Air Force began soliciting him for a follow-on assignment. "Germany was a blast," he said, "but the winters were long and cold...and I needed to get some beach." Thus, the Air Force approved his request for a transfer to Eglin Air Force Base, right in the heart of the Florida panhandle.

Arriving at the 58th Fighter Squadron, JB was elated to see that his unit had the newest F-15C fighters. In fact, these planes were so new that each had less than 100 hours of flight time; and their cockpits had the equivalent of what he called "that new car smell." By virtue of having the newest F-15Cs, the 58th logged several hundred flight hours every month— flying local sorties or deploying to Nellis Air Force Base for any variety of training missions, including the annual Red Flag exercises.[1]

Their regular routine of training, however, was disrupted in December 1989 when Panamanian dictator Manuel Noriega suddenly declared war on the United States. As part of Operation Just Cause, the 58th Fighter Squadron flew combat

---

[1] First held in 1975, Exercise Red Flag is a two-week aerial combat training exercise hosted several times per year by the US Air Force. Its participants include Navy, Air Force, and Marine Corps air squadrons, along with several NATO and Allied air forces.

patrols off the coast of Cuba, lest Fidel Castro dispatch any of his forces to assist Noriega. Fortunately, Castro remained neutral throughout the conflict, and the 58th never had to intercept any Cuban MiGs. But during these nighttime air patrols, Kelk remembered seeing the steady stream of C-130s making their round trips, delivering paratroops and airdrop supplies for their fight against the Panamanian Defense Force. Noriega had no air force to speak of—minus a squadron of 15 attack helicopters and a handful of fixed-wing utility aircraft. Thus, there would have been no opportunities for a dogfight unless the Cuban MiGs had decided to intervene.

But for the men of the 58th, the greatest test of their dogfighting skills would come less than one year later, when they deployed to Saudi Arabia for Operation Desert Shield.

CHUCK "SLY" MAGILL

Chuck "Sly" Magill.

Captain Charles Magill was unique among the flyers in the 58th. By trade, he was a Marine Corps F/A-18 pilot who was on temporary assignment to the 58th Fighter Squadron as part of an interservice exchange program. Born and raised in Wheaton, Illinois, Magill admitted: "I wasn't even interested in the military at first. But I had a neighbor who was an airline pilot, and that seemed like a great way to go." Chuck's grandmother lived near Chicago O'Hare

International Airport and, while going to and from her house, the young lad would often ask his parents to stop by the runway so they could see the airliners land and takeoff. "I just thought it was the coolest thing on the planet," he said, "but it wasn't until I was in college that I realized if you want to be an airline pilot, you probably needed to go into the military." In fact, a disproportionate number of airline pilots were former military.

While attending Arizona State University, he called a local airline company, asking their requirements to become an airline pilot. "You'll need 1,500 hours or an ATP [Airline Transport License]," they told him. "And I didn't know what any of that meant." Still, he enrolled at a local flight school in Glendale, Arizona to earn the credentials he needed for the airline industry. As it turned out, his Glendale flight instructor was an F-4 pilot from nearby Luke Air Force Base who moonlighted weekends as a civil flight trainer. During one of their lessons, Magill recalled taking the airplane over the south rim of the Grand Canyon. While flying this portion of the Arizona countryside, Magill's instructor introduced him to some intense diving maneuvers that certainly pushed the limits of the civil aircraft.

"How do you like this?" the instructor asked.

"This is incredible!" said Magill.

"Well, try doing it at five times the speed. That's what I do. I'm an F-4 driver."

Returning to campus, Chuck began researching each of the service's fixed-wing flight requirements. "The Navy and Marine Corps had guaranteed flight contracts, and the commitments weren't very long. The Air Force wanted to hire me as a navigator. No offense to the navigators, but I didn't want to do that." The Marine Corps' aviation mission, however, fascinated him. The Marines were mostly still using the F-4 Phantom, but their missions seemed to be equal parts "air superiority" and "close air support." Graduating from Arizona State University in 1978, he applied and was accepted into the Marine Corps Officer Candidate program on a guaranteed flight contract. In the spring of 1980, he was on his way to Quantico, Virginia—home of the Marine Corps Officer Candidate School.

"The first couple of days at Quantico were like something out of a movie," he said. "I didn't have a clue what to expect. Nobody briefed me on what to do. I just knew I needed to be at this Quantico place at this time." Although officer candidates weren't allowed to drive their own cars to Quantico, Magill drove his car anyway. He parked it in the officers' parking lot, and proceeded to the in-processing station. "I had long hair, and Izod shirt, and slip-on loafers with no socks." In one hand, he carried his golf bag with tennis racket; in the other hand, he carried a small suitcase. As soon as he walked up the hill to the reception area, he tried to make himself inconspicuous—a monumental task considering his appearance and his golf bag accessories. "And here comes this gunnery sergeant. His name was Claggett, and he was one of the baddest guys I had ever met in my life." Taking one look at the long-hair, loafer-wearing Magill, Claggett exclaimed:

"What the hell do we have here?!"

Magill's "country club" appearance had just made him an unwitting target for the OCS cadre.

Like many, Magill remembered OCS as a culture shock. "I had always made a lot of money as a kid," he said, doing odd jobs and even starting local businesses as a college student. "I worked hard…and had everything you'd think you'd want, except discipline. And OCS was the beginning of real discipline for me." Magill was also impressed by the Marine Corps' mantra that "Every Marine is a rifleman." Indeed, whether a pilot, JAG attorney, or counterintelligence officer, *every* Marine had to qualify with his rifle and learn to maneuver as part of an infantry team.

Although Magill had started OCS on the wrong side of Gunnery Sergeant Claggett's temperament, the OCS experience was somewhat bearable because one of Magill's squadmates was a prior-enlisted Marine who had elected to go the officer route ("Mustangs" as they were called). "He showed me how to spit-shine my boots and how to clean my weapon better than the instructors."

By Week Six, the OCS students had earned the coveted privilege of "weekend passes," which allowed them to venture off base for a weekend of rest and relaxation. "However, if you went out into town, you had to wear slacks. You couldn't wear jeans. It wasn't considered 'officer-like' to wear jeans. But since I had a car, I would take as many of us as I could fit into my Ford Granada and we'd drive up to Crystal City and into Washington, but at the first place we'd stop, about five miles north of Quantico, we'd rip off those khakis and put on jeans and tennis shoes!"

After ten grueling weeks of OCS, Magill graduated with the rest of his classmates. As was custom, the senior cadre gunnery sergeant would render the first salute to his newly-commissioned officer graduates. Giving Magill his first salute, Gunnery Sergeant Claggett said: "Magill, you're a piece of work, but great job."

Before Chuck could attend flight school, however, he would first have to attend The Basic School (TBS)—a six-month training course for all newly-commissioned Marine officers. TBS introduced Magill and his comrades to all facets of the Marine Corps structure and how all other military specialties interacted with and supported the infantry. TBS also put its student officers through a series of tactical field exercises and intense land navigation. "You got to do a lot of live fire; you got to shoot a grenade launcher; and you got to see how the Marine Air-Ground Task Force works." Although comparatively easier than OCS, he nonetheless acknowledged that TBS was no "walk in the park." Upon completing TBS, however, Magill received the orders he had longed to hear: "Report to Naval Air Station (NAS) Whiting Field."

Whiting Field was one of the Navy's two primary training hubs for Naval, Marine, and Coast Guard aviators. Assigned to Training Squadron VT-2, Magill remembered flight school as "really intense." Every day, the students were graded on a variety of tasks in the cockpit and in the classroom. "So, if you have a bad day," he recalled, "you were already falling down in the pack…the lower your grades were, the closer you got to flying helicopters." To be sure, helicopters fulfilled a vital role, but few pilots joined the Marine Corps with the expressed intention of flying them. Typically, flying helicopters was something that a student pilot was *forced* into based on their lower class rankings.

Ironically, though, every one of Magill's Marine flight instructors had been a helicopter pilot—flying either CH-46s or AH-1 Cobras. These chopper pilots had reclassified to become fixed-wing instructors. But when Magill said he wanted to be a fighter pilot, his instructors would say: "Why the hell do you want to be a fighter pilot? You can't support Marines if you go supersonic. You need to be in a helicopter."

But to Chuck Magill, this attitude didn't make sense.

If these guys were so "gung ho" about helicopters, why did they leave the helo community to become fixed-wing instructors? Whatever their motivations may have been, Magill didn't appreciate their antagonistic and seemingly two-faced attitude. By now, however, the Marine Corps had begun transitioning from the F-4 Phantom to the new F/A-

18 Hornet—a fast and agile aircraft that could presumably fulfill the role of an air superiority fighter *and* a ground attack platform. Magill knew that *this* was the plane he wanted to fly.

Despite the bad tidings from his early, helo-obsessed flight instructors, Magill passed flight school with high marks and qualified for a fixed-wing jet billet. His next stop would be NAS Kingsville, where he would learn the fundamentals of piloting jet aircraft. His training mount would be the T-2 Buckeye, a single-engine supersonic jet trainer. A student's performance in the T-2 determined whether they'd go on to advanced jet training aboard the TA-4, a modified training variant of the A-4 Skyhawk. Understandably, each stage of the progressive training was much harder than the last.

"It was like going through a bunch of NFL drafts," he said.

Still, he never lost sight of his desire to fly the F/A-18 and, by the end of his advanced jet training, he had landed high enough in his class rank to have his assignment of choice. The problem, however, was that the Marine Corps would not let novice pilots fly the Hornet until they had earned a few hundred flight hours. Undaunted, Magill stayed at NAS Kingsville as a voluntary flight instructor, racking up his hours until he was eligible to join Squadron VFA-125 for on-the-job F/A-18 training. VFA-125, "The Rough Riders," was the first operational squadron to receive the F/A-18. Throughout the 1980s, it became the *de facto* training hub for all Navy, Marine, and allied pilots who flew exported variants of the Hornet.

It was during these flight sessions with the Rough Riders that Chuck Magill earned his callsign, "Sly." Before a training flight, wherein he would be squaring off against an instructor in a simulated dogfight, Magill complained of having neck pain. The pain wasn't debilitating, he said, but it hurt enough for him to mention it to his evaluator. He added that his performance on the upcoming sortie may be stilted due to his lingering neck pain. During the dogfight, however, Magill easily outclassed his instructor—obtaining "kill shots" that left little doubt as to Magill's burgeoning skill as a fighter pilot. At the post mission debrief, the bewildered instructor (who had probably been expecting an easy victory against a rookie pilot) quickly approached Magill. Despite the latter's neck pain, he had just outmaneuvered a seasoned pilot in a tactical training scenario. "You're a sly dog, Magill," beamed the instructor. "In fact, that's your new callsign: Sly."

Now certified on his dream aircraft, the F/A-18 Hornet, Magill reported to Marine Fighter Attack Squadron 531 (VMFA-531). Over the next four years, he would accrue more than 1,000 flight hours aboard the Hornet and graduate from both the Marine Corps Weapons School and Navy Fighter Weapons School (the famous "Top Gun") and participate in Operation Bright Star—a multi-national training event held in Egypt. During Bright Star, he had the chance to maneuver against Egyptian MiG-21s, which of course made easy fodder for the USMC Hornets.

By the spring of 1989, however, the time had come to select a follow-on assignment. "Everyone knew about the Air Force exchange program," he said. And the program's alumni had commented on how beneficial it was to see the sister services maintain and operate their fixed-wing squadrons. He applied for the exchange program and was accepted with orders to attend Tyndall Air Force Base, Florida, for the F-15 Familiarization Course.

Chuck had heard great things about the F-15 and had read about its exploits in Israeli service against Arab MiGs. There was little doubt that the F-15 Eagle was the undisputed king of the Air Force's fighter fleet. Owing to his experience aboard the F/A-18, Chuck knew his way around the cockpit but, as he noted, the Eagle and the Hornet "were not all that similar...so it required some pretty good study."

When he reported to the 58th Fighter Squadron a few weeks later, he remarked that it was the "best F-15 squadron ever built." He owed much of the unit's esprit de corps to the squadron commander, Paco Geisler, and the cyclic training deployments he offered his pilots. Chuck Magill was confident that, if ever the squadron went to war, he and his newfound Air Force comrades would own the skies wherever they went.

Craig "Mole" Underhill

Born in 1959 in Midland, Michigan, Craig Underhill had a nomadic childhood. His father worked for Dow Chemical—a job that precipitated moves from Michigan to Connecticut to Ohio to California, before landing in Houston, Texas. Ironically, Craig's interest in the military began with the Army. "I had an uncle who was a helicopter pilot in the Army, and my older brother went to West Point." Craig himself had visited the West Point campus on a recruiting visit during his junior year of high school. He was, however, decidedly

Craig "Mole" Underhill.

unimpressed. He opted instead to enroll in the Corps of Cadets at Texas A&M University as a member of their Air Force ROTC program.

Texas A&M was one of the few civilian colleges in America that retained its own Corps of Cadets—essentially a military academy within the larger campus. The cadets lived in their own barracks, retained their own organizational culture, but attended regular classes with the other college students. Virginia Tech was another university with such a program. Although Craig wanted to be a pilot, he was first commissioned as a navigator in December 1981.

Although the training pipeline for navigators was shorter than it was for pilots, navigators received more hours of classroom instruction. For the young Craig Underhill, these training sessions took place mostly at Mather Air Force Base near Sacramento, California. Classes included topics on radar navigation and celestial navigation. "It was a great experience for me and I'm glad I did it. I ended up being a C-130 navigator, which was a great mission for a young navigator." In fact, serving aboard a C-130 gave him the opportunity to factor load plans and Drop Zones into his navigational calculus.

It wasn't long, however, before Craig decided to try again at becoming a pilot. Because he was already a navigator, the transition to pilot was pretty seamless. He already knew how the planes operated and he could find his way around the cockpit. UPT did, however, have its challenges. The T-37, for instance, was one of the most asinine planes he had ever flown. "I really struggled with those," he admitted.

But the T-38 was a different story.

The false starts he had had with the T-37 evaporated as soon as he took control of the T-38. His performance in the latter was so good, that he landed in the top echelons of his class at UPT, earning him a slot to FLIT and finally the

F-15 Familiarization Course.

Learning to pilot the F-15, he said, was "very tough." The fighter community "wants you to be the best air-to-air guy you can be." Understandably, the learning curve was steep. The F-15 Eagle was, after all, the most-advanced fighter jet in the world, capable of reaching Mach 2.5 while fully-loaded with eight missiles and could still pull 9Gs in a turning dogfight. "The course required a lot of self-study," he said, but all the instructors wanted their students to succeed.

Around this time, Craig also came by his callsign, "Mole"—a creative play on his name. Someone in his unit decided that a mole was a fearsome animal who could maneuver "under hills," and thus Craig was anointed as "Mole." The callsign stuck for the remainder of his career.

Arriving at the 58th Fighter Squadron in August 1988, Craig was impressed by the quality of the unit and the caliber of its leadership. He was assigned as Rico Rodriguez's wingman and, like his fellow pilots, Craig enjoyed the numerous training missions and deployments the 58th received. These brand-new F-15Cs needed to be "broken in" and he was happy to push the envelope during mock dogfights and air patrols over the Gulf of Mexico. By the time Iraq invaded Kuwait in August 1990, Mole had logged nearly 350 hours in the Eagle, and was a two-ship flight lead.[2]

LARRY "CHERRY" PITTS

Larry Pitts was another victim of a callsign that was derisively inspired by his last name. Cherries have pits; thus "Cherry" became his *nom de guerre*. Born in Washington state in 1956,

---

[2] In Air Force parlance, fighter jets are called "ships" when referring to flight formations. Thus, a flying formation with two airplanes is called a "two-ship" formation. A "flight lead," as the name implies, refers to the pilot who is the designated leader of that formation.

Larry "Cherry" Pitts.

he spent his formative years growing up in the suburbs of Anchorage, Alaska. He was a few years older than most of his contemporaries in the 58th because, ironically, he began his career as an Army helicopter pilot.

In the aftermath of Vietnam, and amidst the transition to an all-volunteer force, Pitts took advantage of the generous flight incentives that the post-war Army was offering. He thus became a Warrant Officer pilot in 1976, flying Hueys out of Fort Ord, California. When he left the Army in 1980, he decided that there was more of a future in flying fixed-wing aircraft. He thus approached the local Air Force recruiter and presented his credentials as an Army helicopter pilot. Not surprisingly, Pitts was soon on his way to OTS, arriving at

Lackland Air Force Base in November 1982.

His Army background had prepared him well for the mental and physical rigors of OTS. But the Air Force was a different branch of service, with a different mission, and a different culture. Still, he enjoyed learning the unique aspects of life in the Air Force. It was hard to deny, however, that the Air Force had nicer facilities and demonstrably better funding. Even during the darkest days of the post-Vietnam era, the Air Force didn't seem to suffer quite as badly as its sister services had done. The Air Force, simply by virtue of *being* the Air Force, was never as hard-up for quality recruits. Perhaps it was the panache of the aerial missions, or the prospect of lucrative post-service careers in aviation technology.

Completing OTS, Larry reported to UPT at Williams Air Force Base in Arizona. Given his helicopter background, UPT was relatively easy for him. He did, however, have to learn the nuances of fixed-wing instrumentation, and how their flight dynamics differed from rotary-winged aircraft. Following UPT, Larry took his first assignment as a T-38 flight instructor.

After being selected for and certified on the F-15 Eagle, Larry reported to the 58th Fighter Squadron in 1989. He would stay with the squadron for nearly *nine* years. "This was when General McPeak was the Air Force Chief of Staff," he recalled. McPeak's mantra was: "There's an officer for every assignment. So, if you don't want to move, you don't have to." Families loved this idea, as it would give them more stability, and presumably allow them to set down roots in the local communities. For those stationed at Eglin, the Air Force dependents welcomed the prospect of homesteading on the Gulf Coast of Florida—enjoying the beach life in nearby communities such as Destin and Fort Walton Beach. For the airmen, however, McPeak's policy hamstrung their opportunities to grow professionally.

Yet in August of 1990, Pitts and his wingmen would receive the greatest "growth" opportunity of their careers: deploying to Saudi Arabia for a showdown with the Iraqi Air Force.

Tony "ET" Murphy

Born in Los Angeles and raised in small-town Oregon, Tony Murphy grew up with a deep-seated fascination for jet aircraft. Like many of his comrades, he had earned a private pilot's rating during his teenage years, cutting his teeth on the normal variety of Cessna and Piper aircraft. "I didn't have any

Tony "ET" Murphy.

plans to go to college," he said, "I just wanted to fly jets." And he solicited each of the Armed Forces recruiting offices with the same inquiry: "I want to fly jets."

First, he went to the Air Force recruiter.

"I want to fly jets."

"You can't fly jets," said the recruiter.

Then he went to the Navy recruiter.

"I want to fly jets."

"You can't fly jets," said the recruiter.

Then he went to the Marine recruiter.

"I want to fly jets."

"You can fly jets but you've got to enlist first."

Then he went to the Army recruiter.

"I want to fly jets."

The Army told him about helicopters.

"I kept badgering the recruiters until finally, the Air Force said: 'You need to go to college first.' Now we were getting somewhere."

After graduating from high school, Tony attended the local community college for one year before transferring to Oregon State and enrolling in the Air Force ROTC program. Upon entering the program, he repeated his stock phrase:

"I want to fly jets."

"Are you sure you want to fly jets?" his ROTC commander asked him.

"Look, I'm getting a degree in mechanical engineering, I've got a private pilot's license, and I want to fly jets!"

"We can help you out."

The 1980s were an interesting time to be an ROTC cadet. Many of the senior cadre were Vietnam veterans and were elated to see the increase in military spending. Moreover, they were elated to see an American public growing less antagonistic towards its military.

"So, I went through the normal ROTC program, passed the physical, and they said: 'Ok, we're going to give you a chance to fly.' My commander at the time, Don Karpen, gave me a break since I didn't have the best grades and I wasn't exactly your model military guy. He got me an assignment to Shepperd Air Force Base, Texas, for pilot training, which gives you good chance to fly fighters afterwards. That was my first big break."

Reporting to Shepperd for UPT, Murphy noted that he had "dynamite instructors"—men who knew how to distill the complexities of jet aviation and put the course material into terms that the student-pilots could easily digest. "They taught me what I needed to know in the best way they knew how, plus they were fun to fly with." Although Murphy mastered the basics of the T-37 and T-38, he admitted that: "I was not the best guy in the class by far." In fact, his class standing had guaranteed him a follow-on assignment as a UPT flight instructor. But, at the eleventh hour, one of his flight commanders intervened to secure him a FAR designation. "I don't know what his reasons were, but that was my second big break."

It was during UPT that he unwittingly earned the callsign "ET." One night, after frequenting a local bar with many of his UPT classmates, Murphy had to call his wife for a ride home. His classmates, seeing Murphy at the payphone, razzed him for "phoning home…just like ET!" Thus, it came as little surprise when his callsign ceremony ended with the bestowment of "ET" as his *nom de guerre*.

With his FAR endorsement in hand, Murphy contemplated his next move. "Assignment blocks at that time of year always seemed to be heavy in Eagles, so I ended up getting an F-15 to Eglin Air Force Base, Florida. I was pretty darn happy with the Eagle, as you can imagine, but Chris, my wife, wasn't too pleased about Eglin since Florida wouldn't accept her pharmacy license. I didn't know much about Eglin, but I heard it was a nice place and the Eagle's a great jet. I ended up in the squadron with a good friend, Bruce Till [callsign: "Roto"], who had been with us since UPT."

Murphy recalled that by the time the Gulf War started, he and Till had been flying at Eglin for nearly two and a half years, "and we were already working on our next assignments." Indeed, by the summer of 1990, ET Murphy was a four-ship flight lead and had logged several hundred hours in the F-15C. "The noteworthy point about those two and a half years," he said, "was the near constant TDYs [Temporary Duty] to Red Flag. We were always at Nellis Air Force Base in Las Vegas. You can imagine the good large-force exercises and the awesome training we got from all those trips. We even called the war 'Rag Flag' because our training was so close to the real thing."

MARK "NIPS" ARRIOLA

Mark Arriola, Chuck Magill's wingman, was among the youngest pilots in the squadron. A 1987 Air Force Academy graduate, Mark was the son of a private pilot and had come from a long lineage of civil aviators. "I grew up around it," he said. And one of his earliest mentors while growing up in Washington state was a fighter pilot neighbor who was then stationed at McCord Air Force Base. "His name was Frank Wright…he flew F-102s and F-106s." As a young lad, Mark enjoyed hearing Wright's tales of derring-do from the cockpit of the Century-series fighters. When Mark graduated from the Air Force Academy, his neighbor Wright administered the commissioning ceremony. And when Mark graduated from UPT, Wright pinned his old silver wings on Mark's uniform.

Mark "Nips" Arriola.

During his time at the Air Force Academy, Mark noted that several of his instructors and commanding officers were Vietnam veterans, or had flown high-profile missions during the post-Vietnam era. One of his Air Officers, Commanding (AOCs), for example, had been a C-130 pilot during Operation Eagle Claw—the failed attempt to rescue American hostages in Iran. His C-130 had carried a handful of the surviving members back to friendly airspace.

At the Air Force Academy, the flight selection process was quite different than it was for the OTS graduates. "It was all based on your military performance and your grade point average," said Mark. He knew he wanted to be a pilot, but he was amenable to flying *any* category of aircraft. During the summer before his junior year, however, he had the opportunity to train with an F-15 squadron at Tyndall Air Force Base, wherein he logged several flight hours in the backseat of an F-15B. "From that moment forward," he said, "I was going to do anything and everything I could to fly that airplane." And after four years of hard work at the Academy, Mark was both elated and relieved to discover that he had been selected for UPT.

After completing UPT, FLIT, and his F-15 certification, Mark reported to Eglin Air Force Base as one of several new lieutenants assigned to the 33d Fighter Wing—the 58th Fighter Squadron's parent unit. "It was interesting because the 33d Fighter Wing, at the time, had three squadrons—the 58th, 59th, and 60th. And at any one time, those squadrons rotated through what was called the 'Alpha Squadron' status. The Alpha Squadron was the one squadron that, if there were a need for a rapid deployment, that squadron would be tasked to do it." As fate would have it, the 58th Fighter Squadron had been the designated "Alpha" since April 1990, and would hold that status for six months—just in time to receive the alert for duty in Saudi Arabia.

BILL "TONIC" THIEL

Lieutenant Colonel Bill "Tonic" Thiel assumed command of the 58th Fighter Squadron on April 9, 1990—taking over from "Paco" Geisler. Although Bill admittedly had "big shoes" to fill, he was nevertheless an accomplished fighter pilot. Born and raised in the dairy farmlands of Wisconsin, Bill came of age during the inspired patriotism of the Eisenhower-Kennedy years. Growing up on a farm and "being outside all the time, I could see the airplane contrails in the sky and that always fascinated me about airplanes. Of course, as I grew

Bill "Tonic" Thiel.

older, the military seemed like the best way to break into the flying game."

Although Vietnam was in full-swing by the time Bill graduated from high school, it did not dissuade him from enrolling in the Air Force ROTC program at the University of Wisconsin—Madison. "I was lucky enough to fight for and get an ROTC scholarship during my sophomore year. Plus, they paid you fifty bucks a month, which was a lot of money back in the late '60s."

But campus life in the 1960s was by no means idyllic. "Vietnam demonstrations were starting to reach fever pitch in 1968-69," said Bill, "you know, Students for a Democratic Society [SDS] and other radical demonstrators." In fact, during the summer of 1970, some rabid protestors had blown up the Army Mathematics Research Center on the UW-Madison campus. Things were getting so bad that ROTC programs across the country were ordering their cadets *not* to wear their uniforms on campus.

UW was no exception.

"It was a pretty tough time to be in the military. We weren't well-liked on campus." But social unrest and domestic politics aside, Bill Thiel enjoyed his time in the UW ROTC program. Upon passing his pre-flight physical examinations, the young Thiel was selected for pilot training when he graduated from UW in 1971. "The Air Force needed pilots because Vietnam was still going pretty hot and heavy. In that regard, I hit the window just perfectly."

By the time he reported to UPT, he was already a private pilot, having earned his license aboard a Cessna 152 during his college years. After UPT, however, Bill spent the first four years of his flying career (1972-76) as a flight instructor. Although pilot slots were still plentiful in the early 1970s, Thiel's UPT class came up short on fighter assignments. "There were only two fighter slots available," he said—both of which were on the F-4 Phantom II. "There were a few more slots for the RF-4 [the reconnaissance variant of the Phantom] and a handful of slots for the A-7 Corsair." The rest of the available slots were for heavy aircraft like the B-52 and C-130. Wanting to hold out for a fighter slot, and not keen to the idea of piloting a "heavy, crewed aircraft," Bill elected to stay at UPT as a T-37 and T-38 flight instructor.

It was a wise career decision, as it gave him hundreds of hours in additional flight time before transitioning to fighters in 1976. By now, the Air Force had brought the F-15 Eagle online and were training the first of its fighter crews. It was during Thiel's time in FLIT that he came by the callsign "Tonic." His FLIT class took an unusual approach to meting out callsigns. Whereas most FLIT classes gave each other callsigns based on unflattering events or circumstances, Bill's class was allowed to select their own callsigns. "Gin and Tonic was my drink of choice," he said, "and so I thought about 'Gin,' but that didn't seem appropriate, so I picked 'Tonic' and that stuck with me. And when I got to my first operational assignment at Bitburg, they let me keep it!'"

Bitburg Air Base was prime posting for a Cold War fighter pilot. The operational focus centered on the defense of Western Europe and, every week, Bill and his comrades took to the skies defending NATO's airspace. Whether running aerial patrols over the East German border, or responding to the intermittent "scramble" alerts, Tonic Thiel enjoyed flying over the Frontier of Democracy.

On one occasion, Bill got to see how the other half lived. During an annual exchange program, wherein the East German military chaperoned a NATO delegation into East Berlin, Bill was allowed a supervised visit into the capital city. East Berlin was, by all accounts, an Orwellian nightmare come to life. "Cameras on every corner," he said. "People on the streets wouldn't look at you, wouldn't talk to you. We got to do some shopping, but they [the East German chaperones] wouldn't let you buy much. And when you went into the stores to purchase anything, it was strictly matter of fact—no conversations allowed or anything like that. It was really eye-opening to see how people behind the Iron Curtain lived at the time. When we got back across the border, it really made you appreciate what we had in the West."

Flying F-15s at Bitburg Air Base from 1980-84, Bill returned stateside with orders to the Air Force Inspection Safety Center in northern California. Although it was a critical job to the Air Force's mission, and gave Bill responsibilities above his paygrade, it was still a "staff job" that afforded him no flying time.

Luckily, he wouldn't have to wait long to get back into the cockpit.

After a follow-on assignment as the Chief Safety Inspector for NATO air units at the Keflavik Air Base in Iceland, Bill landed at Eglin Air Force Base with the 60th Fighter Squadron. Two years later, he assumed command of the 58th.

Barely four months after taking the reins from Paco Geisler, Bill awoke to the startling news that Iraq had invaded Kuwait.

JOSE "CHIEF" MATOS

Chief Master Sergeant Jose Matos was destined to be a world-class aircraft mechanic. Throughout the 58th's deployment to Desert Storm, Matos and his miracle-working crew chiefs kept the squadron at a 98% readiness rate—a feat that was

Jose "Chief" Matos.

unheard of even during peacetime. Like many modern-day heroes, Jose Matos was an unassuming man from humble upbringings. Born in Orocovis, Puerto Rico in 1948, he was the eldest of seven children. "We grew up poor and there was no money for school."

There was, however, a rich tradition of military service in the Matos family. A US Commonwealth since 1898, all Puerto Ricans were American citizens by birth, and many had served with distinction in World War II and Korea. Among these Puerto Rican GIs was Matos' father, a ten-year Army veteran. Realizing that military service was the best means of upward mobility for his son (but not keen to recommending the Army), the elder Matos suggested the Air Force. Jose already had a long-standing interest in aviation. As a boy, he had caught a glimpse of a cover story in the January 1957 issue of *Life Magazine*—"Around the World in 45 Hours"—showcasing the Herculean feats of the B-52 Stratofortress. Matos also had a cousin working at Ramey Air Force Base (on the northwestern edge of the island) who could facilitate the enlistment. "On May 2, 1968, I drove through the gates of Ramey Air Force Base, and I enlisted."

Reporting to Lackland Air Force Base for Basic Training, Matos took readily to the military lifestyle. He had been a gifted athlete in high school, and his Spartan upbringing in the central highlands of Puerto Rico had prepared him well for the hardships of military training.

"My biggest problem," he said, "was English."

Aside from a few conversational words and phrases, Matos spoke virtually no English. Many Puerto Rican servicemen had struggled with the same. Although English was a "co-official" language in Puerto Rico, it had long taken a backseat to Spanish, with the latter being the preferred language for nearly 95% of the residents.

Apart from the language barrier, his most memorable

moment in Basic Training occurred on June 5, 1968. Matos and one of his fellow trainees were cutting grass outside the barracks when, suddenly, the other trainee started crying.

"What's going on?" Matos asked.

His friend related that Bobby Kennedy had been shot earlier that morning.

Matos started crying, too.

"I remember where I was when JFK got killed. And now his brother was dead, too." To men like Jose Matos, political assassinations were the province of Third World dictatorships, not free and prosperous societies like America.

Meanwhile, the political climate surrounding Vietnam had gone from bad to worse. Riots and protests had intensified over the last two years, and President Johnson had promised to find a solution to the conflict. Still, America was losing more than 1,000 servicemen every month in a conflict that was growing ever more unpopular at home. When Matos reported to Sheppard Air Force Base for flight mechanic training, he knew that he would eventually end up in Vietnam.

Be that as it may, Matos nevertheless enjoyed learning about the complexities of aircraft maintenance. It was a highly technical trade—and the skill sets were in high demand throughout the aviation industry. "Another thing that impressed me the most was the first time I got paid as an airman. I reported to the pay sergeant and he put $72 in my hand [$548.02 in 2021]. That was the most money I had ever had in my life at the same time."

But the pay and benefits didn't get to the heart of the matter. Matos genuinely had a passion for his work. While improving his English, he spent hours studying the inner workings of planes like the F-4 Phantom II—the workhorse in the skies over Vietnam. At his first operational assignment at Shaw Air Force Base, South Carolina, Matos found himself in the Repair & Reclamation Shop. Each maintenance unit had a variety of "shops"—each of which were responsible for a different aspect of maintenance on the planes. Repair & Reclamation, as Matos recalled, was essentially "crash recovery…our responsibility was to recover aircraft," most of which had crash-landed on final approach or had suffered in-flight malfunctions. "And we were also responsible for major repairs."

By 1972, Jose Matos was a buck sergeant and was approaching his window to re-enlist or return to civilian life. His skills as an aircraft mechanic would carry over nicely into the maintenance shops at United Airlines or Pan Am, but Matos wasn't ready to leave the Air Force yet. That spring, he re-enlisted with orders to Cam Ranh Air Base in Vietnam.

Although by 1972, the war in Vietnam was ostensibly "winding down," Matos saw a very different picture from the air base at Cam Rahn Bay. Aside from the countless hours repairing and refitting the planes coming back from their sorties, the base itself was a frequent target for North Vietnamese rocket fire. Enemy troops lingering in the night would fire their 122mm rockets from beyond the perimeter, hoping to hit an Allied aircraft or one of its crewmen. Luckily, Matos survived these close encounters with enemy rockets and, the following year, the US announced its final withdrawal from Vietnam.

Matos, by now a staff sergeant, returned stateside with orders to Eglin Air Force Base, where he held a variety of jobs supporting the resident fighter squadrons—including Flight Line Expeditor and Quality Assurance Inspector. In 1978, however, the Air Force selected Matos and forty of his squadron mates to attend the introductory maintenance course for America's newest fighter jet: the F-15 Eagle. "That's where my F-15 career started," he said, "that course at Luke Air Force Base in 1978." Casting his eyes upon the first-production Eagles, Matos was awestruck. The F-15's powerplant, avionics, and general construction was a marked improvement over the latter-day F-4 Phantom.

After the new F-15s arrived at Eglin, Matos had the chance to see their destructive power at the William Tell Competition in 1984. Every two years, the Air Force selected its best fighter squadrons to compete in the aerial gunnery exercises at William Tell. The competition included a series of both gun and missile engagements. Matos beamed as he watched his F-15s sweep the competition at William Tell for 1984 *and* 1986. In fact, it was during the 1986 competition that he received a phone call from the squadron commander, informing him that he had been promoted to chief master sergeant, and that he was next in line to become the Squadron Maintenance Chief. This promotion would put him in charge of all maintenance aspects for the twenty-four F-15Cs in the 58th Fighter Squadron.

Chapter 2

EASTBOUND

As news of the Iraqi invasion spread, many didn't know what to make of Saddam's aggression. Some pilots dismissed the invasion as just another "Arab conflict"— they expected the Gulf crisis to run its course without their involvement. Others were excited by the prospect of going to war. After years of squaring off against mock aggressors during the annual Red Flag exercises, they would finally have a chance to prove themselves in combat. Others had cause for concern. Aside from the brief interludes in Panama and Grenada, the US hadn't seen a full-scale conventional war in nearly twenty years. With memories of Vietnam still fresh in their minds, many older pilots wondered if the US had the political fortitude to withstand another high-intensity conflict. Others were simply dumbfounded. Still, every man in the squadron remembered where he was, and what he was doing, when he learned of the Iraqi invasion.

For Rick Tollini, it was just another August morning. "I walked into the squadron bar for a coffee and a smoke," he said. "I was a closet smoker back then. I am not sure why I ever started. Maybe I was bored, or just felt a little rebellious and wanted to do something 'different,' but once I started, it sure was hard to stop. But, for now, a morning smoke and a cup o'Joe was what I needed. What I saw that morning on

TV as I walked into the Gorilla bar/break room made me quickly realize I had 'picked a bad day to quit smoking' (to quote *Airplane*)." Indeed, as Rick sallied into the bar, he was flagged down by his friend, Larry "Cherry" Pitts.

"Hey, check this out!" said Larry.

Fixing his eyes onto the barroom TV, Tollini saw the CNN breaking newscast, rolling footage of some fully-loaded F-15s from the 1st Fighter Wing at Langley Air Force Base—"taking off and heading toward Saudi Arabia." The headline stated that Iraq had just invaded Kuwait, and President George HW Bush had ordered an immediate response. "Holy crap!" thought Tollini. "It only made sense that if this potential contingency operation expanded, the Eglin F-15s would be next 'on call.'"

For Chuck Magill, there was no question that the 58th Fighter Squadron would deploy. "We had been called in for Operation Just Cause," he said, "so there was no question that we were well-prepared." In fact, Magill was surprised that the 1st Fighter Wing at Langley had been called to deploy before the F-15s at Eglin.

Magill and a few of his comrades had just finished their rotation to Exercise Maple Flag, an annual air exercise hosted by the Royal Canadian Air Force in Cold Lake, Alberta. Similar in scope to the annual Red Flag exercises, Maple Flag hosted several NATO partners and other Allied air forces. During Maple Flag '90, Magill had flown alongside American F-16s and Canadian-modified CF-18 Hornets. Returning to Eglin on July 30, 1990, he never expected that Iraq would invade Kuwait three days later.

"The Iraqi invasion didn't matter to me," he said. All told, Chuck wasn't the least bit scared. He had flown against Arab pilots and Arab MiGs during the Bright Star exercises, and was not impressed by their skills or their equipment.

Bill Thiel concurred. When he first heard of the Iraqi

invasion, his thoughts immediately harkened back to his days as a T-38 instructor pilot. "At the time, we had a lot of foreign pilot trainees, most of whom came from Iran and Saudi Arabia." Indeed, the Shah of Iran and the House of Saud routinely sent their air force pilots to be trained in America. "I had some experience training these Middle Eastern pilots and most of them, to be frank, weren't very capable. They needed a lot of extra rides to get through the program." These foreign students couldn't be dismissed unless they were qualitatively a hazard to themselves or others. "Their sponsor country wanted them to fly until they got it right." Still, he felt chagrined because UPT would frequently dismiss American students who couldn't pass their check rides, but gave numerous attempts to the Middle Eastern students who were, at best, marginally capable within the cockpit. Bill felt that many of the American "washout" students could have passed UPT had they been given the same second chances that the foreign students had received. These sentiments were echoed by many of the naval flight instructors who had trained Iranian F-14 pilots at Miramar, California. These instructors had said that their Iranian students were more interested in "driving Corvettes and chasing skirts" than learning to fly the F-14.

Given Bill's experience in training the Saudi and Iranian pilots, he understandably had low expectations for the Iraqi Air Force. "They had some state-of-the-art equipment," he said, "but I had no reason to believe that their pilots were as good as their equipment."

Mark Arriola wasn't so sure. "They had us outnumbered four-to-one in terms of total aircraft." Still, he knew that the Iraqis relied heavily on Ground-Control Interception (GCI) radars. Moreover, the Iraqi training programs tended to discourage initiative-taking and exercising independent thought. "They were basically being told when, where, and how to fly," he added. The men of the 58th knew that their own tactical bearings gave them an advantage, "but the one thing we couldn't overcome," said Arriola, "was sheer numbers." For if the Iraqis could send *that* many airplanes aloft, "it was going to be a lot more challenging for us."

Craig Underhill, too, was shocked by the invasion. But given the reputation of the 58th Fighter Squadron, and the collective skill of its pilots, he was *convinced* that they would deploy. In fact, the Gorillas were somewhat of a "dream team" among the USAF fighter squadrons. "We had Weapons School instructors; we had regular instructors; we had mission commanders"—and a whole slew of qualified section leads. "We were hoping we'd make the cut," said Craig. But given their collective expertise, and their performance during Red Flag and Operation Just Cause, the bigger question for Craig Underhill was: "How could we *not* deploy?"

Larry "Cherry" Pitts, meanwhile was on temporary assignment to Bitburg, Germany, showing the European-based F-15 squadrons some new, experimental tactics that the 58th had been developing at Eglin. For Pitts and his wingmen at Bitburg, "we didn't think too much about the invasion. We still had another week before we were scheduled to come home, so we spent that week travelling around Austria, enjoying ourselves after being in Germany for a month." Larry didn't think he would deploy, otherwise the 58th would have called him home straight away. Flying back to Eglin the following week, however, he could tell from the activity on the flight line that a deployment was imminent. He had come home just in time.

Cesar Rodriguez, likewise, thought little of the invasion, at first. After all, the squadron's Area of Responsibility (AOR) was Eastern Europe. If ever the Cold War suddenly turned "hot" on the European mainland, the 58th Fighter Squadron would be on the frontlines of NATO's air war. To this point, the Gorillas had spent most of their time studying the tactics and organization of the Eastern Bloc air forces. But now that the Cold War was over, the squadron had no AOR and no focused mission beyond their cyclic training sorties.

All told, Rodriguez didn't have much time to think about the invasion. For within days of that CNN broadcast, he and a few of his wingmen were on their way to another training exercise, this time as mock aggressors for the Missouri Air National Guard.

This Guard unit, however, was still flying the F-4 Phantom.

Although they were slated to receive the F-15 Eagle, the Air National Guard commander wanted to hold one final F-4 vs F-15 showdown.

By now, however, the Phantom's best days as a fighter were behind it. Even the F-4 "Wild Weasel" variants were approaching the twilight of their careers. And the outcome of this F-4 Phantom/F-15 Eagle matchup only confirmed the Phantom's obsolescence. Outnumbered two-to-one, the F-15s pulverized the Air National Guard F-4s in one tactical scenario after another. "It had nothing to do with their airmanship," said Rodriguez. Indeed, the F-4 drivers were all competent pilots, many of whom had flown on active duty. The F-15 was simply *that* much better of an aircraft.

But when Rico and his comrades landed following the exercise, they were greeted by an urgent communique from the 58th, ordering their immediate return to Eglin. "So, before anybody could start popping beers," he said, "I had to get everyone back together, get the maintenance troops lined up, go back to our rooms, and pack our bags."

From the brevity and urgency of the message, Rico could tell that something was up.

"We landed at Eglin just after sunset," he said. On his final approach and taxi, however, he noticed that the squadron hangar bays were fully illuminated and bustling with activity. The other F-15s in the squadron were being loaded with

reserve ammunition and fitted with external fuel tanks—
"everything that you needed for going into combat." All this
activity could only mean one thing: *the 58th Fighter Squadron
was going to war.*

But whatever their thoughts or predictions, the same
question lingered on many an airman's mind:

"What was Saddam thinking?"

As it turned out, Saddam Hussein had carefully calculated
the risks and determined that the odds were in his favor. He
was certain that his army (the fourth-largest in the world) and
his air force (the largest in the Middle East) would make short
work of any rescue force that came to liberate Kuwait. He
wagered that the Americans would lead a military response
against Iraq but, as he famously quipped, America was "a
society that cannot accept 10,000 dead in one battle." Indeed,
the memories of Vietnam were as galvanizing to Saddam
Hussein as they were disheartening to the American public.
He was confident that after the Americans had suffered a few
thousand casualties, they would sue for peace on Iraq's terms.

Saddam Hussein rose to power in 1968 following the Ba'ath
Party revolution. As vice-president under Ahmed Hassan Al-
Bakr, Saddam introduced a number of popular reforms—
including the nationalization of Iraqi oil and promoting free
education. As Al-Bakr's health declined during the 1970s,
Saddam gradually became the *de facto* ruler of Iraq. However,
as he ascended to the presidency, Saddam ruled Iraq with a
brand of brutality reminiscent of Hitler and Stalin. He
nevertheless seemed poised for a long and prosperous rule of
Iraq until his fortunes changed in the wake of the Iranian
Revolution.

Fearful that the Ayatollah's rhetoric would galvanize Iraq's
Shiite majority, Saddam preemptively invaded Iran on
September 22, 1980. The ensuing Iran-Iraq War would last

eight years and ended in a bloody stalemate that claimed more than 300,000 Iraqi dead. Aside from the untold cost in human suffering, the conflict left Saddam straddled with a multi-billion-dollar war debt, most of which had been financed by Kuwait. But rather than pay his debt to the Kuwaiti government, the "Butcher of Baghdad" simply invaded his neighbor to the south. To justify the invasion, Saddam reignited the long-standing border dispute between the two countries. He also made false allegations that the Kuwaitis had been slant-drilling Iraqi oil and that they were deliberately trying to keep the price of oil low by producing more than OPEC's set quotas. Kuwait held ten percent of the world's oil reserves and generated 97 billion barrels of crude each year. Thus, Saddam reasoned that if he could not repay his debt, he would simply annex the tiny emirate and take over its petroleum industry.

In the days leading up to the invasion, satellite imagery revealed several thousand Iraqi troops massed near the Kuwaiti border. On July 25, 1990, US Ambassador April Glaspie met with Saddam Hussein to discuss the sudden mobilization. Aware of his increasingly hostile rhetoric in the border dispute with Kuwait, Glaspie stated:

> "We can see that you have deployed massive numbers of troops in the south. Normally that would be none of our business, but when this happens in the context of your threats against Kuwait, then it would be reasonable for us to be concerned. For this reason, I have received an instruction to ask you, in the spirit of friendship—not confrontation—regarding your intentions: Why are your troops massed so very close to Kuwait's borders?"

Saddam assured the ambassador that he was committed to finding a diplomatic solution. In his conversation with Glaspie, Saddam informed her that Egyptian leader Hosni Mubarak had arranged for Kuwaiti and Iraqi delegations to meet in Riyadh and that more negotiations were scheduled in Baghdad. Moreover, he relayed to Mubarak that "nothing serious will happen" with Kuwait before the negotiations began.

Glaspie concluded her meeting with Saddam by stating that the US had "no opinion" of Arab-Arab conflicts such as the border dispute with Kuwait. "All that we hope," she said, "is that these issues are solved quickly." But for Saddam Hussein, the only quick solution was to destroy the emirate of Kuwait.[3] Thus, on the morning of August 2, 1990, more than 100,000 Iraqi troops and several hundred Iraqi tanks stormed across the border, the spearhead of an eighty-mile blitzkrieg into Kuwait City. Encountering only piecemeal resistance, Iraqi tanks thundered into the heart of the Kuwaiti capital, assaulting the city's central bank and carrying off with its wealth. A coordinated air-ground attack decimated the Dasman Palace, home to Kuwait's ruler Emir Jabel al-Amhad al-Sabar. The emir himself and a few members of his staff barely escaped with their lives as they fled Kuwait by helicopter. The last transmission made over the state-run radio network was an appeal for help.

What truly shocked the international community, however, was the sheer barbarity of Iraq's Army. At times, it seemed that Iraqi soldiers were torturing Kuwaitis simply for their own amusement. Tank crews randomly fired their guns into places of commerce while other soldiers loaded their cargo trucks with various items of loot, laughing and shouting "Ali Baba! Ali Baba!"

The United Nations responded by issuing their normal

---

[3] Following the invasion, Glaspie drew fierce criticism for her remarks, with many accusing her of giving Saddam tacit permission to invade Kuwait. However, she acted entirely within State Department protocol. American diplomats do not have license to make threats or implications of military force. Also, per State Department policy, the US does not take sides in border disputes between two of its allies.

variety of condemnations. Economic and military sanctions soon followed while President Bush authorized the first US deployments to the region. On August 6, 1990, elements of the US XVIII Airborne Corps received their orders to the Persian Gulf. Within days, the aircraft carriers *Saratoga* and *Eisenhower* were steaming towards the Persian Gulf while coalition air squadrons began pouring into Saudi Arabia by the hundreds. This first wave of deployments became known as "Operation Desert Shield"—a deterrent against Saddam Hussein lest he try to invade the Kingdom of Saud.

Watching the crisis unfold from their homes and breakrooms at Eglin, the men of the 58th readied their F-15s for combat. When Rico Rodriguez returned from his exercise with the Missouri Air National Guard, he was given swift orders: "Go inside, get a quick intel update, and start packing your bags for an indeterminate amount of time." By now it was clear that they were deploying to the Persian Gulf, but none of them knew how long they would be there. Saddam's forces were digging in along the Saudi border and, at present, he remained undeterred by the international condemnations.

But for the 58th Fighter Squadron, the bigger problem, it seemed, was simply tacking down a date for their deployment. Tollini described it as a "constant yo-yo of up and down deployment warnings then cancellations. It was nerve racking, because one minute we would be 'leaving tomorrow,' then the next it would get cancelled with an expectation of leaving in another week's time. Or it would be, 'We might never deploy, so don't get too excited.'" During these tense days, Rick Tollini said "Goodbye" to his wife and daughter at least four different times.

ET Murphy found himself in the same conundrum. "In that whole shuffle, there were five days when we had to sit by the phone just in case the plan changed again. Poor Chrissy [his wife], she was about ready to kick me out the door because I was frustrated and getting on her nerves. That was a very common feeling. What do you talk about when you're supposed to stay in your house, but you're going to war? That was an emotional roller coaster."

While tempering their thoughts on the Gulf crisis, however, the pilots received numerous intelligence briefings on the Iraqi Air Force (IQAF). Following the invasion, every news outlet had reported *ad nauseam* that Iraq had the world's fourth-largest army, but little had been said about their air force. "Our intel teams put together some packets for us," said Rodriguez—intelligence handouts explaining the size, structure, disposition, and tactics of the IQAF. Not surprisingly, the IQAF had much in common with the latter-day Soviet Air Force. For that matter, much of their aircraft had been supplied by the Soviet Union. Soviet trainers and advisors were frequent guests at Iraqi airbases, and many Iraqi pilots had attended flight schools in Russia.

As Rick Tollini recalled, many of these intelligence briefings were recaps of lessons learned from the Iran-Iraq War. The geopolitical irony, however, was that each side had been trained and equipped by two competing superpowers—the US and the Soviet Union. But although the Iraqi and Iranian air forces were well-equipped by their respective allies, neither had matched the flying skills nor the technical expertise of their benefactors. This partially explained why neither the Iraqis nor the Iranians could decisively defeat one another, even after eight years of combat. "We knew they had some capabilities," said Tollini, "but I also knew that they weren't able to fight us on our level."

Still, eight years of combat experience and strength in numbers were hard to ignore. Cherry Pitts echoed Mark Arriola's earlier concerns about fighting outnumbered in the skies over Iraq. "We thought that, because of the amount of combat they had seen against Iran, that they'd be a pretty capable air force. They had a large number of airplanes. And they had quite a few fourth-generation fighters, including the MiG-29. Most of us thought that we'd probably lose *some* airplanes just based on the sheer number of fighters they had." As Joseph Stalin said: "Quantity has a quality all its own."

The Iraqi MiG-21s and MiG-23s, however, were of little concern to anyone. By 1990, the MiG-21 was an outdated fighter and it had easily fallen prey to the F-4 Phantom in the skies over Vietnam. Its avionics and maneuverability posed no threat to the F-15. The MiG-23 was likewise derided. Although a decent interceptor, it was a generation behind the current inventory of American fighters. The MiG-25 was a threat only in terms of its speed. In a turning dogfight, however, it was sure to be the loser.

The MiG-29, however, was a different story.

Known by its NATO Reporting Name: "Fulcrum," the MiG-29 was essentially the Soviet Union's answer to the F-15. Entering service in 1982, the MiG-29 had been exported to numerous Arab and Eastern Bloc air forces. Considering its performance data and onboard avionics, the Fulcrum was sure to give the Eagle a run for its money in a dogfight.

Another potential adversary was the French-built Mirage F1. Given their ties to the Middle East, Dassault Aviation exported nearly 90 Mirage F1 fighters to the IQAF. These specially-designed export variants were dubbed the "F1EQ," with Iraq being the sole recipient. Even though the F1 couldn't outmaneuver an F-15 or F-16, Mirage fighters nevertheless stood head-and-shoulders above any third-generation MiG.

But as far as Bill Thiel was concerned, the greater threat lay in the enemy's surface-to-air missile (SAM) batteries. The Iraqis' air defense network had a slew of Soviet-built SAMs, each of which could cause considerable damage to an F-15.

In fact, one technique that the Iraqis had used to great effect was the so-called "SAMbush," wherein Iraqi fighters would go airborne to draw enemy bandits into a pursuit, leading their pursuers right into the engagement envelope of a SAM battery waiting below.

But for as tough as the IQAF appeared on paper, their training and maintenance programs were primitive by NATO's standards. A war against Iraq, if and when it came, would not be won through air power alone, but an aerial campaign could certainly disrupt the IQAF and soften up Saddam's ground forces. Still, some anticipated fighting a horrendous battle in the deserts of Iraq. Defense analysts and other "experts" were anticipating as many as 20,000 casualties on the first day of the ground war. And this estimate didn't take into account what would happen after coalition forces met the Republican Guard—Saddam's elite ground troops.

The biggest threat, however, came from Saddam's chemical weapons—especially Sarin and Mustard Gas. Saddam had used both chemical agents against the Kurds and the Iranians, the effects of which were seen by the squadron through raw documentary footage. The pilots and ground crews, however, had received extensive training on how to prepare for a chemical/biological attack. In the air, an F-15 could easily outrun (or fly above) any chemical attack. Even the deadliest strands of Mustard Gas couldn't rise more than a few hundred meters above ground level. On the ground, however, an airmen's first line of defense against a chemical agent was his M17 protective mask. In the event of a chemical attack, an airman had only *nine seconds* to properly don and seal his mask before succumbing to the surrounding gas agents. The M17 would filter out any harmful air, and retain the airman's vital functions, but would do nothing to save his exposed skin from harm. Thus, if time permitted, the airman could also don his chemical protective suit, a rubber outer garment lined with charcoal to neutralize any chemical agents on the airmen's skin or uniform. Although US intelligence had estimated that the likelihood of a chemical attack was small, the men of the 58th were well-prepared to fight against it.

As preparations continued, Chief Matos and his maintenance crews were perhaps the busiest of all. A few days after receiving the deployment alert, Matos and his crews learned that the squadron would be occupying King Faisal Air Base in Tabuk, Saudi Arabia. On the diplomatic front, the US had successfully negotiated the use of several airbases within Saudi Arabia to accommodate the growing Allied coalition. The airbase at Tabuk belonged to an F-5 Tiger squadron of the Royal Saudi Air Force (RSAF). "We had four KC-10s on standby," said Matos. The KC-10 was an aerial behemoth that could double as a transport *and* an in-flight refueler. Each KC-10 would be loaded to capacity with the various hardware needed to maintain the squadron during its deployment. Because these maintenance assets needed to be in place by the time the F-15s arrived at Tabuk, Chief Matos and his aircraft handlers would have to arrive with the "Advanced Team"—flying ahead of the main body and setting up shop to receive the F-15s after completing their transatlantic flight.

Throughout most of his time with the 58th, Matos' right-hand man was Master Sergeant Todd McGirr. As the Maintenance Production Supervisor, McGirr was responsible for scheduling and coordinating maintenance operations among the various crew chiefs and technicians that serviced the planes. Each F-15 had a dedicated crew chief; the mechanics and technicians were parceled out from the various support sections. Understandably, maintaining a squadron of F-15s was a multi-layered process, requiring a synchronized effort across several maintenance sections.

As McGirr described it, much of the direct support for the F-15s occurred on the flight line. "Day-to-day operations," he said, "are run by critical maintenance elements that operate the on the flight line with a series of vehicles." Indeed, each maintenance section had its own truck that carried their equipment to the flight line—be it for fixing radars, weapons, or engine components. The crews jokingly referred to these vehicles as "bread trucks," given their resemblance to the latter-day Mrs. Baird's delivery vans.

Matos had brought McGirr onto his maintenance team due to the latter's experience as a private pilot. "So that knowledge actually helped me a lot when it came to troubleshooting flight control problems and things like that," said McGirr.

Like every man in the squadron, McGirr was shocked to hear of the invasion, but he wasn't surprised when the 58th was alerted to deploy. "We were glued to our TV sets when it first started happening," said McGirr. "Then, the very next thing they showed on TV was Langley [1st Fighter Wing] loaded for bear and heading out. We knew we were next." After all, there were only so many F-15C squadrons that could handle a mission of this magnitude. McGirr also noted that the F-15s of the 58th Fighter Squadron carried the APG-63 radar system, one of the most powerful airborne radars of its day.

Meanwhile, the pilots continued readying their F-15s for deployment. Of course, prepping the F-15 for a transatlantic flight was no easy task. Across the anticipated fourteen-and-a-half-hour flight, there would be at least *ten* aerial refuels. Prior to takeoff, every component of the F-15s' powerplant and avionics would be inspected for potential problems. The maintenance crews would fix any issue that could even *slightly* disrupt the F-15s' journey. During long flights such as these, pilots typically followed a pre-concocted "diversion plan," allowing them to land at any nearby airfield if they suffered an in-flight malfunction. But for this pending transatlantic flight, the nearest emergency landing strip would be at Lajes Air Base in the Azores—nearly 800 miles off the coast of Portugal. Ejecting over the Atlantic Ocean was the *last* thing any pilot wanted.

All things considered, this transatlantic flight was guaranteed to be unpleasant. Although the F-15's cockpit was roomy by the standards of fighter aircraft, fourteen and a half hours in a single-seat fighter would take its toll on anyone. There would be no in-flight movies; no music playlists; and virtually no room to stretch. Beyond the token radio calls from his wingmen and the various air traffic control stations, the pilot would have no one to talk to. Moreover, at certain altitudes, the blue tinges of the sky would blend with the colors of the ocean below—creating a virtual "wall of blue" beyond the canopy. Similar to a motorist who becomes hypnotized by the passing yellow lines, a pilot would have to fight to stay focused as the monochromatic blue horizon passed underneath his wings.

Although they were given orders to pack for an "indefinite amount of time," the single-seat F-15C could only accommodate so much storage. The small storage area behind the pilot's seat was known as "Bay Five"—large enough to hold three to five carry-on bags. "We stocked some oddball stuff," said ET Murphy. "We received messages from the advanced team to bring things like liquid soap and lots of toilet paper." Arab culture, after all, was not known for using either. "We also picked up a sling shot for rats." Indeed, while occupying the billets at Tabuk, the Advanced Team reported having to chase out rats and other vermin. "We thought that there were rats all over the place so we might as well have some target practice," Murphy continued. "We figured whatever was on the jets [F-15s] was going to have to hold us over for a while." Hence, the pilots packed their chemical protective gear along with as many personal bags as they could fit into their Bay Fives. Among the more notable items crammed into Bay Five were the ubiquitous Meals Ready to Eat (MREs). The MRE was a self-contained field ration sealed in a lightweight slip package. Delivering more than 1,000 calories per meal, the MRE featured sealed entrees such as spaghetti, beef stew, and normally had three side courses, including a dessert. Though not a fancy or even fulfilling meal, it was a step up from the canned rations of the Vietnam era. Still, the MRE was a frequent target of ridicule among American servicemen—often referred to as "Meals Rejected from Ethiopia" or "Multiple Rectal Explosions."

As preparations continued, the 33d Fighter Wing made the painful decision that some of their more junior pilots would be left behind. These younger lieutenants were only a few months out of FLIT and had not yet completed their MQT time. Specifically, the Wing leadership decided that any pilot with less than 300 hours of flight time on the F-15 had to remain at Eglin. As it turned out, Mark Arriola was one of only *three* second lieutenants in the squadron to meet the flight time requirements. "There were two other lieutenants besides myself: Scott 'Papa' Maw and Robert 'LA' Brooks," said Arriola. "We were essentially the 'bottom three' lieutenants. Each of us just barely had over 300 hours."

To backfill the pending personnel losses, the 33d Fighter Wing temporarily reassigned a handful of seasoned pilots from the 59th and 60th Fighter Squadrons to the 58th. The influx of new personnel brought the 58th Fighter Squadron's manning roster to a total of thirty pilots. The squadron itself, however, had only twenty-four F-15s. As a rule, every fighter squadron deployed to combat with more pilots than aircraft. High manpower ratios were necessary for a squadron to keep its jets in the air on a 24-hour rotational basis.

And no one was happier than Bill Thiel to receive these incoming personnel.

As it were, his fellow squadron commanders had given him

their "best and brightest"—including the top-ranked flight
leads and weapons officers from their respective units. "We
got three pilots from the 59th Squadron, and seven from 60th
Squadron," said Thiel. One of the incoming replacements
from the 59th Squadron was Captain Rhory "Hoser" Draeger.
Hoser was the Weapons Officer for the 59th Squadron and
had recently become an eight-ship flight lead. His hard-
charging style of airmanship and uncompromising standards
for training had earned him a reputation as one of the fiercest
fighter pilots in the Wing.

Considering that much of the IQAF had recent combat
experience in their own backyard, it made sense for the 33d
Fighter Wing to leave their lesser-experienced pilots at home.

Understandably, none of these younger pilots were happy
with the decision.

"They were heartbroken," said one thoughtful comrade.

These young Eagle drivers were anxious to see combat.
Now, they felt as though they'd be missing "The Big One" of
their generation. But as fate would have it, many of these
young fliers went on to see action during the "No Fly Zone"
missions, and in the skies over Bosnia.

For the F-15 pilots at Eglin, the cyclic anticipation finally
ended on the evening of August 25. That night, Bill Thiel
received final confirmation that the facilities at Tabuk were
ready, and the squadron would deploy the next morning.
Although they were ostensibly going into harm's way, Tonic
Thiel and his wingmen had an unshakable confidence in
their skills and their equipment: "Thanks to the Reagan years,
the US fighter community, I felt, was as well-equipped and
well-trained as it had ever been. We were just coming off our
deployments to Red Flag and Maple Flag, so our readiness
was really high. We always exceeded the Air Force standard to
have 85% of our aircraft 'Mission Capable' at any given time.

That was also helped by the fact that our aircraft were all fairly new. We had one of the newest versions of the F-15C at the time. It's like a new car; they're always in great shape for the first 40,000 miles or so. But they don't stay that way if you don't have good maintenance people…and we had a *great* maintenance team."

On the morning of August 26, 1990, six flights of four F-15s prepared to depart Eglin Air Force Base. Within the next twenty hours, each of the squadron's twenty-four F-15s would touch down at the Tabuk air base. Their flight plan would take them through a long and laborious route, adding additional miles to avoid the projected hurricanes and tropical storms brewing in the mid-Atlantic. As Rico recalled: "We would be flying up the East Coast, past Charleston, then across the Atlantic to the Straits of Gibraltar, through the Mediterranean, then down through the Suez."

While shaking off his frustration from the earlier false starts, ET Murphy recalled: "I was so busy getting ready for the real departure brief that I didn't get much of a chance to say goodbye to Chris. She grabbed me some lunch at Burger King and gave it to me just as the brief started. All I could do was give her a quick kiss and say: 'See you in a couple months, maybe, I hope.' That was our goodbye." By this point, Murphy and his wingmen had covered the departure brief at least twice, so the information was, as he put it, "just a review."

But just then, as they prepared to climb aboard their planes, it started to rain.

The downpour wasn't bad enough to warrant cancelling the mission, but it was bad enough to aggravate the pilots who were still packing their personal gear into Bay Five. "We needed lots of time to arrange the two box lunches, luggage, Walkman, tapes, the flight plan, and all that stuff," said Murphy. "But it was pouring. What a mess."

As ET Murphy took off in his four-ship flight, he

bound** 63

immediately had problems with the cooling and pressurization system. The F-15's cockpit was a fickle mistress, and even the most detailed pre-flight maintenance checks couldn't prevent the occasional "gremlins" from working their way into the Eagle's onboard systems. "It was hotter than heck in my cockpit," he said," with the cabin pressure fluctuating—not exactly something you want to cross the pond with." His ears didn't appreciate the constant fluctuations in cabin pressure but, after the first aerial refueling, he was happy to report that: "My problem cleared up and the jet ran fine for the rest of the trip."

Most of the pilots had already made transatlantic flights— going to and from Germany during their normal rotations along the Iron Curtain; or going to and from Egypt during the annual Bright Star exercises.

This time, however, they were going to war.

And the wartime exigencies meant a slightly longer time between aerial refuels. Given that many of these rendezvouses were happening over the Atlantic, each linkup had to be perfectly timed and coordinated. For if any fighter missed his refuel point, or suffered a mechanical failure that prevented him from tethering to the fuel line, he would have to eject over the Atlantic Ocean.

Most of their transatlantic flight occurred during the non-daylight hours. Because the planes were travelling east, they were flying away from the setting sun, and they "lost" hours with each passing time zone. "We were over the Mediterranean when the sun came up," said Murphy. "Africa, with the sand and the beautiful coast, drove home the fact that we were in a different part of the world."

But as the F-15s made their final stretch across the Mediterranean, their pilots were understandably tense. They would soon be crossing over Muammar Al-Gaddafi's "Line of Death." Larry Pitts recalled that: "We left our radars turned off during most of the flight, but not when we flew by Libyan airspace." The so-called "Line of Death" had been a flash point between the US and Libya for most of the 1980s. The term "Line of Death" referred to an arbitrary line that Gaddafi had drawn over the Gulf of Sidra—claiming it as Libya's territorial waters. Although Gaddafi had no legal basis to make that claim, he frequently sent the Libyan Air Force to interdict any American warships that crossed his imaginary Line of Death. Twice during the 1980s, American F-14s shot down hostile Libyan aircraft over the Gulf of Sidra. Tensions remained high, and the pilots in the 58th were told to expect harassment from Libyan MiGs. "But," as Larry Pitts said, "it turned out to be a 'nothing burger.'"

The F-15s flew over the Gulf of Sidra without incident. "We really knew we were headed for someplace different when we crossed the Nile and part of Egypt," said Murphy. The F-15s then vectored down the Suez Canal, making their final approach into Saudi airspace. "Our base was in the northwest corner of Saudi Arabia," Murphy continued, "not far from the Red Sea and just a few miles south of Jordan."

Crossing into the Kingdom of Saud, however, each of the pilots were relieved to discover that they would *not* have to fight their way into the country. There were no lingering Iraqi bandits or hostile recon flights in the area. Still, just a few hundred miles away, the IQAF and the Iraqi Army stood menacingly over the ravaged emirate of Kuwait.

Meanwhile, back at Eglin, Rick Tollini and Craig Underhill were among the few pilots in the squadron who were not selected to make the solo transatlantic flights. Because the squadron now had thirty pilots against twenty-four F-15 Eagles, six pilots would inevitably have to hitch a ride on a C-141 transport. Once in country, the six additional pilots would be designated "airborne spares"—essentially "floaters" who would hop into whatever F-15s were available after the incoming pilots entered their mandatory rest cycles. It was this manning procedure that allowed the squadron to send sorties aloft on a continuous, 24-hour basis.

At first, Underhill was disappointed by not taking the solo F-15 flight, but admitted that the C-141 was both roomy and comfortable. Years later, after completing eight transatlantic flights in a solo F-15, Underhill was glad to have ridden the C-141 into Saudi Arabia.

But simply getting to Saudi Arabia seemed to be a task unto itself. "The deployment plans for so many different squadrons, personnel, and equipment trying to get to the Southwest Asia Theater," said Rick Tollini, "had taxed both airlift and tanker assets." Tollini himself had been on the manifest for the Advanced Team, and he had anticipated arriving at Tabuk in the first wave of personnel from Eglin. But, as he noted: "My airlift flight ended up being diverted to another base, and then a layover at Dover AFB." From Dover, Tollini had to change planes, climbing aboard a roomier C-5A Galaxy. "We got to ride in the 'first-class' seats in the upper deck area," he chuckled. "We ended up getting into Saudi Arabia a good day-and-a-half after our jets and other pilots arrived at Tabuk. So much for planning ahead."

But Tollini admitted that these flight delays were bearable because he kept good company—most notably the squadron flight surgeon: Captain Cory Cornum. Affectionately known throughout the unit as "Doc Cornum," he was a likeable fellow and fiercely loyal to his pilots. "He had brought plenty of 'supplies' with him," said Tollini, "and that included some little blue pills called Restoril. He handed them out to myself and the other pilots to ensure we arrived 'fresh' in-theater." Restoril was typically used to treat insomnia, but it was one of the few medications that had become a regular part of the Air Force pharmacopeia. Flight surgeons would often give it to their pilots as a sleep-inducing agent, thus ensuring that the air crews slept during their mandatory rest cycles. Throughout the Air Force, Restoril was known colloquially as a "no-go pill." Conversely, amphetamine and dextroamphetamine were given as "go pills" to keep air crews awake and alert during their long hours of flight time.

"I don't recall much of the long multi-layover flight," Tollini continued, "because I had a great sleep along the way." In the days ahead, Kluso Tollini remarked that: "I would come to appreciate how much Doc Cornum was able to use his medical expertise to keep myself and all the other pilots fully combat ready regardless of our operations tempo." Coincidentally, Cory Cornum was married to an Army flight surgeon, Major Rhonda Cornum. "Rhonda would later be shot down over Iraq on a combat rescue mission and captured by the Iraqis." Years later, she co-authored a book about her experiences in the Persian Gulf, titled *She Went to War: The Rhonda Cornum Story*.

As the front ramp of the C-5 opened, Tollini and his comrades could feel the dry heat of the high desert. They were the last of the Eglin personnel to arrive at Tabuk, and they took a healthy gaze at the place they would call "home" for the next several months.

Chapter 3
TABUK

Chief Matos was among the first to land at Tabuk. But as he started downloading gear from the first KC-10, he was shocked to see that *none* of his maintenance teams had yet arrived. Indeed, amidst the chaos of trying to scramble personnel into theater, the Air Force had placed his maintenance teams onto a follow-on flight of C-130s. And although these planes were *expected* to arrive at the same time as Matos, some logistical hiccups had delayed their departure from Eglin.

Matos was livid.

All twenty-four of the squadron's F-15s would be arriving soon, and he had *no* available personnel to ferry the incoming jets to their shelters or conduct their post-flight maintenance.

Undaunted, Matos simply grabbed whatever personnel he could find, and put them through a proverbial "crash course" on how to perform post-flight maintenance checks on the F-15. He grabbed one Air Force security policeman and said: "Listen, I'm going to show you how to check some things on the airplane," including oil pressure and vital systems checks. Matos then grabbed a nearby cook, dressed him the standard maintenance coveralls (colloquially known as a "bunny suit"), and showed him what to look for when inspecting the F-15's air intakes post-flight.

When the F-15s finally arrived at Tabuk, Matos and his two novice helpers (the cook and the security policeman) were, at first, the only ones performing post-flight maintenance on the F-15s. Soon, however, Jose Matos found another unexpected helper in the form of an American contractor. "Learjet had the maintenance contract for Tabuk," he said. "So, you had Air Force civilians working for Learjet and managing the Saudi F-5 operations." One of the American contractors, seeing that Matos was horribly understaffed, came over and said:

"How can I help?"

Matos directed him to service the F-15s' Liquid Oxygen (LOX) Equipment. The LOX systems provided clean oxygen to aircrews at altitudes above 10,000 feet. "And he serviced my LOX," said Matos. "Of course, it took several hours to inspect, service, and fuel all the airplanes. When you gas up an F-15 with *three* external fuel tanks, it's going to take a lot of fuel."

It would be several more days before the rest of Chief Matos' maintenance teams arrived at Tabuk. But reflecting on the impromptu help he received from the cook, the security policeman, and the contractor, Matos said: "Those guys saved my ass! If I had done that post-flight maintenance all by myself, it would have been *very* difficult."

On his final descent into Tabuk, Rico Rodriguez realized just how much his lower body had atrophied after several hours in the cockpit. "Everything from my hips on down was pretty much asleep. Stopping the jet was a bit of a challenge because you had to use those muscles to apply the brakes." Rico, like many of his comrades, had to be slowly carried out of the cockpit by the ground crews. After the long transatlantic flight, an egressing pilot had to be physically supported by his comrades on either side, helping him walk as the normal flow of blood returned to his legs.

Once Rico regained his footing, he handed the F-15 off to his crew chief and ambled over to his designated billet. After spending several hours in the air, he was now entering the mandatory "crew rest" cycle. Every flying unit kept its flight crews on a strict cycle that mandated how many hours they should rest between sorties. The problem, however, was that many pilots had trouble "shutting down" even after coming off long missions—hence the rationale behind "go" and "no-go" pills. Pharmaceuticals would regulate a pilot's sleep cycle whenever his own physiology failed to do so.

The billets and accommodations at Tabuk were impressive by Western standards. "We doubled up two to a room," said JB Kelk—not uncommon for a military setting. During their first month at Tabuk, the pilots and crewmen stayed in what Kelk described as "dormitory-style" billets with community bathrooms at the end of every hall. "About a month later," he said, "we moved into these little pseudo-apartments"—still two to a room, but each suite had a shared bathroom.

Chuck Magill was likewise impressed by the amenities at Tabuk. During Operation Bright Star in 1985, he had been sleeping in tents. These dormitory-style billets were like five-star resorts by comparison. And he was elated to discover that his assigned roommate was Doc Cornum. It was perhaps the closest thing to having his own personal physician nearby.

As Chuck Magill and Mark Arriola emerged from their F-15s, they noticed that their Saudi hosts had organized a small celebration in the mess hall. "We got out of the jets," said Mark, "and the Saudis had a little gathering for us"—a welcoming feast, of sorts. "I had never seen anything like this in my life," he continued, "but these Saudi officers were sitting around on the floor and they all had their hands dug into this goat carcass! And they're just pulling meat off this carcass...eating with their hands." Mark and Chuck just looked at each other and grabbed as many items from the nearby fruit bar as they could carry—"because I was not about to go putting my hands in a goat carcass after a fourteen-and-a-half-hour nonstop flight."

Chuck agreed.

"The food was awful," he said. "I became a vegan for the next nine months. We just weren't used to eating goat or lamb...and the meat was always filled with bone pieces." Of course, they had a full complement of MREs, but an airmen could only live off MREs for so long before developing digestive issues. Thus, Magill and many of his comrades opted for the naturally-grown fruits, vegetables, and salads.

Bizarre meals notwithstanding, Tabuk had everything the squadron needed for its daily operations, including stable runways, hangars, and maintenance facilities. Said Todd McGirr: "On the base, we dispersed our airplanes initially into four parking areas, and we gave each of them names: Center Stage; Death Valley; Circus Circus; and Disneyland." Center Stage housed most of the maintenance assets. Whenever an F-15 returned from a sortie, its destination parking ramp depended on the plane's operational status. "When the pilot was coming back," said McGirr, "he would call us at about 50 miles out, and he'd give us the status of the airplane so we could get the maintenance teams ready." The incoming pilot would give his status based on a numeric code. "Code 1" meant that the plane was fine; no issues detected. "Code 2" was a nuisance problem, meaning that the pilot could fly the plane again, but with potential impact to his mission capabilities. A "Code 3" problem, however, was enough to ground the plane upon its return. Code 3 maintenance issues typically included engines, oil, avionics, radars, and weapons suites. "The squadron lived and died by the Code 3 problems," said Chief Matos. Once on the ground, Code 3 planes would go to Center Stage. Code 2s would be diverted to Death Valley or Circus Circus. Code 1s would go directly to Disneyland for immediate refuel and post-flight maintenance checks before being handed off to the next pilot coming out of crew rest.

For the aircraft hangars, Todd McGirr recalled that they were so small that the F-15s had barely twelve inches of wing clearance from either side of the hangar walls. "They had been built to accommodate F-5s," which was a much smaller plane than the F-15 Eagle, "but the structures were adequate for our needs."

When Rick Tollini arrived at the Tabuk Air Base, he took note of its unique location—"just southeast of the Israeli–Jordanian border." As Tollini recalled: "Tabuk had a closer straight-line distance to Baghdad than any other US unit in Saudi Arabia." This meant that the squadron could fly more round-trip missions into the combat zone with fewer re-fueling. I made sure the combat plans people understood this, to our benefit."

As the rest of the squadron settled into Tabuk, they began prepping the F-15s for what would become a nonstop, 24-hour mission cycle. Crew manifests were carefully constructed to ensure that every plane had a pilot, and that every pilot was gainfully employed. Some pilots would go airborne while others would rest. When the airborne pilots met their maximum flight hours, they would swap out with those who were resting. Come what may, the 58th would have planes in the air twenty-four hours a day during the opening months of Desert Shield.

As the military coalition grew, Lieutenant General Chuck Horner (USAF) became the commander of Allied air forces. At his command were more than 2,500 tactical aircraft—1,800 of which were American. The remainder came from a smattering of allies including France, Canada, and the United Kingdom. It was, by all measures, the largest aggregate air force since World War II.

In the opening months of Operation Desert Shield, American F-15 pilots flew aerial maneuvers similar to what they would experience in combat. However, US Central Command Air Forces (CENTAF) initially kept their F-15s on a tight leash. Indeed, one of CENTAF's earliest restrictions was to limit the Allied sorties to a minimum altitude of 300 feet. Meanwhile, CENTAF and coalition leaders created the Tactical Air Control Center (TACC) in Riyadh to plan and organize the air campaign against Iraq.

The 58th's daily operations were governed by the all-encompassing Air Tasking Order (ATO), delivered every morning by TACC to all in-theater air units. Because this was 1990, however, the ATO arrived by Learjet and was presented on a floppy disk, from which the squadron would have to print multiple hard copies. When the ATO arrived, Bill Thiel remembered that it contained instructions for *every* air unit in theater. "We had to break out our portion of the ATO," said Thiel—determining their assigned air patrol sectors, times on station, and fuel allocations. After culling the necessary data from the ATO, the designated flight leaders would construct the day's flight plan.

Throughout Desert Shield, the squadron's daily flight plan consisted mainly of High-Value Airborne Asset Protection (HVAA)[4] or Defensive Counter Air (DCA) missions. HVAA missions provided fighter escort to such high-value assets including the E-3 Airborne Warning and Control System (AWACS); the EC-130 Airborne Battlefield Command and Control Center (ABCCC); the RC-135 Rivet Joint

---

[4] Pronounced "have-uh"

reconnaissance aircraft, and the KC-135 Stratotanker. "Each of these assets," said Rico Rodriguez, "were trying to gather information on the enemy"—and monitor any changes to the disposition of Iraqi forces. "We were up there protecting them within 24 hours after landing at Tabuk."

DCA missions, on the other hand, were designed to intercept any Iraqi aircraft that attempted to probe the Saudi border. Before every mission along the Saudi-Iraqi border, the pilots would receive a pre-departure brief, whereupon the intelligence staff gave the latest updates on the disposition of Iraqi forces—including what aircraft were flying and which airfields had been the most active.

One of the featured players in this ongoing game of cat-and-mouse was the MiG-25. The Soviet-built interceptor was known for its exceptional speed, but poor maneuverability. As Chuck Magill recalled: "The MiG-25 had the turning radius of a refrigerator…something like 18 miles." During their regular reconnaissance sorties, the Iraqi MiG-25s would trace the border at speeds of Mach 2.5. In fact, speed was the MiG-25's best defense. It had outflown Israeli F-4s during the Yom Kippur War, but had fallen prey to Israeli F-15s in the skies over Lebanon. "We knew that the Iraqis were using MiG-25s for intel collection," said Tollini—trying to assess the disposition and capabilities of the burgeoning Allied coalition.

Whenever a MiG-25 sortie appeared on CENTAF's radar, a flight of F-15s would vector to run interference. The rules of engagement, however, prohibited firing on Iraqi aircraft unless they violated Saudi airspace. "We saw a lot of aircraft up there," said JB Kelk, "but the one that concerned us the most was the MiG-25 because it can fly high and very fast, so it made for a very challenging intercept profile." Typically, the MiGs would turn away as soon as they realized an F-15 had acquired them on radar.

Another frequent visitor to the Saudi borderlands was the Mirage F1. During a routine DCA mission, Bruce "Roto" Till was the first pilot in the 58th Fighter Squadron to make contact with an Iraqi F1. That afternoon, Till was the flight lead of a formation that included Larry Pitts and Bill Thiel. "We were getting information all the time from the AWACS," said Till. And the latest readings indicated that two Iraqi bandits were flying close to the border.

No surprises here, thought Till. Border-tracing flights were typical for the IQAF.

But these incoming bandits were taking a more aggressive flight pattern than he had seen on previous missions. "It looked like they were getting ready to cross the border, which was a big 'no-no.' Based on their incoming speed and aspect, you could tell the AWACS were getting a little concerned about this." Of greater concern was that these bogeys would vector to take down the AWACS itself.

Roto then took a hard right on the throttle, bringing his F-15 parallel to the Iraqi border. Now tracking the bogey with his onboard radar, Till was shocked to see the leading Iraqi jet cross the border into Saudi airspace.

"The AWACS gave us clearance to fire."

Vectoring northeast to meet the incoming bandit, Till was about to get a radar lock when the Iraqi F1 suddenly changed course. Perhaps the wayward bandit realized he had crossed the border, or realized that he was now on Till's radar. The F1 then jinked into a hard-left turn which temporarily took him out of Till's missile range. But by the time the Iraqi pilot came out of the turn and sped northward, he was already back across the border—thus robbing Till of his anticipated missile shot.

"That could have been the first kill of the war," he said.

But because the bandit had returned to Iraqi airspace, he

was no longer a "threat" and could not be engaged.

As Till's wingman, Larry Pitts had likewise been ready to fire on the elusive bandit. "No kidding, my thumb was on the way down to fire that missile when the AWACS called us off." He then watched helplessly as the fleeting bandits disappeared from his radar. "Not that we cared, but it was very important to CENTAF that if we shot something down, the wreckage needed to land in Saudi Arabia."

Although these probing sorties could be a nuisance, the 58th knew that the Iraqis were dependent on GCI systems. This essentially put the Iraqi planes on a tether for maintaining good situational awareness, as none of their onboard avionics could match the range or capabilities of NATO-based aircraft. Still, "the Iraqis had a pretty well-integrated air defense system," said Tollini. The IQAF had divided its homeland airspace into different sectors, "and they had an air defense command in charge of those sectors," Tollini added. In fact, this knowledge had influenced CENTAF's planning process during the early days of Desert Storm, targeting different sectors and developing contingencies based on how the Iraqis might react.

For most pilots, though, these early MiG sightings were few and far between. Typically, these bandits would trace the border from a distance of 10 miles, then turn away as soon as their onboard warning systems alerted them to a nearby F-15. "But they were testing us, too," said Rick Tollini. "They wanted to see how we responded to their flights and their provocations. That was normal, even during peacetime"—referring to the borderland intercepts of Soviet aircraft at the edge of NATO's airspace.

When they weren't chasing off lingering MiGs and Mirages, the pilots of the 58th spent considerable time refining their night flying tactics. "We had to get used to flying with our lights off," said Rick Tollini, "and flying under radio silence." Under these conditions, a pilot had to rely on nothing more than his onboard instrumentation. These intense nighttime maneuvers were something that the 58th Fighter Squadron had never done before. "Night training in the F-15 community was almost nonexistent at that point," Tollini continued. "Nobody liked flying at night," he said, "and typically we would train maybe one or two missions at night, every three months." But to seize the initiative and maintain the element of surprise, American F-15s would have to own the night.

To refine their nighttime airmanship, however, the 58th returned to basics. In the F-15 community, the standard nighttime formation consisted of a two-ship element (i.e., the flight leader and his wingman) spaced at a distance of 2-5 nautical miles. The problem, however, was that this formation was better suited for defensive operations; it didn't translate well into the offensive-planning mindset nor did it permit optimal use of firepower.

The squadron, therefore, adopted Rick Tollini's recommendation to use a modified variant of the standard daytime formation. Known as the "Wall of Eagles," this daytime formation placed four F-15s flying abreast covering a distance of five nautical miles. The nighttime modification, as Tollini described it, "was a little bit wider than a normal daytime formation just to assist with flight path deconfliction and to reduce the workload on the wingman spending time on formation management." This doubled the formation's length from five nautical miles to ten.

"I decided early on in our night training," said Tollini, "that my 4-ship element would attempt to practice and validate the ability to fly a nighttime 'wall' formation without night-vision goggles (NVGs) or Fighter Data Link (FDL)."

It was a daunting task, but the pilots were up to it.

Thus, without NVGs, every pilot would use the lowest setting on his navigation lights to maintain visual contact with the other planes. "We also had contingency lighting options to quickly regain sight of each other by a communicated request or by whatever tactical action we were performing at the time," Tollini continued. "For example, a request to 'Flash' meant for the other flight member to momentarily turn on their bright-red, anti-collision lights, which could be seen from far away. Or, a 'burner' call meant that somebody had just engaged his afterburner, which was also very noticeable from far away." But these contingency options were only to be used in case of emergency, as they could easily expose their position to the enemy. As soon as the formation was within ten miles of the objective, the pilots would cut off their navigation lights, flying in total darkness with nothing to guide them except the "big sky theory" (i.e., hoping that the airspace was big enough to negate the possibility of any mid-air collisions). Then, too, the ambient light from the exchange of gunfire and missile blasts would likely provide *some* illumination in the dark.

The Squadron Intelligence staff, meanwhile, continued gathering as much relevant data as they could find regarding the IQAF. Updates to the IQAF's disposition and air movements were published daily. "Everybody used every resource available to help us build situational awareness of what could be up there," said Rico Rodriguez, "and the current Russian capabilities that were there." Given the ties between Iraq and the Soviet Union, Rodriguez and his wingmen expected to be flying against Russian pilots at some point during the air campaign. "So, we planned for the worst; and then planned again on top of that."

Meanwhile, Rick Tollini, as the Weapons Officer, stayed busy planning how the squadron would cover its daily taskings from the ATO. "I had to come up with plans and options how best to cover the Quick Reaction Alert (QRA—or scramble alert) we had been tasked to perform," he said, along with organizing the mission plans for the cyclic DCA patrols.

On his first night at Tabuk, he had been looking forward to having a full night's sleep, when suddenly he awoke to the sound of someone pounding on his room door. "I was barely able to come out of my stupor," he recalled, "as I saw the outline of somebody standing over my bed."

It was Colonel Rick Parsons, commander of the 33d Fighter Wing.

"Even though we had deployed as a single squadron," Tollini explained, "with Tonic as our deployed squadron commander, Colonel Parsons had also deployed with us." Given his rank, Parsons had become the deployment commander by default.

Parsons wasted no time. "Kluso, Kluso ... are you awake?"

Still sleepy-eyed, Tollini muttered: "Yes sir. I think so?"

"Okay, you need to get dressed and out on the ramp by 0300."

Looking at his watch, Tollini was not amused to see that it was currently 2:30 AM. "There's a C-21 [Air Force Learjet used for liaison missions] coming to pick you up and take you to Riyadh," Parsons continued. "They are having a big planning conference there and they need somebody from the 58th to represent us. I'll drive you out to the flight-line. Are you ready to go?"

Sleepily, Tollini acknowledged: "Yes sir. I'll be ready in 5 minutes."

Grabbing a small flight bag, he quickly stuffed it with some underwear, socks, an extra flight suit, and his toiletry kit. "I was ready, I guess." As Parsons took him to meet the incoming Learjet, he said he did not have much information about what the meeting would cover, but advised him to use his "best judgment" and to brief him upon his return. With a quick "Yes sir!" Tollini jumped on the C-21, touching down in Riyadh less than two hours later.

On the tarmac, Tollini met a staff liaison officer who took him to a four-star hotel in Riyadh. Once there, Tollini was issued a blanket and pillow, before being ushered into a huge ballroom that had been converted into a sleeping area lined with nearly 500 cots, many of which were occupied by sleeping US servicemen. The liaison officer told him he would be back at 8:00 AM to pick him up for the briefing, "so I was able to get about an hour of sleep and a great buffet breakfast on-the-house." Indeed, the breakfast buffet was a welcomed change from the MREs and raw animal fare at Tabuk. "Fresh eggs, bacon (yes, bacon in Saudi Arabia), and great coffee…it was the only time I would be lodged to that level of comfort for the next five months."

At 8:00 AM, the same staff liaison picked him up for the short drive to the RSAF Headquarters compound, which had now become the impromptu headquarters for CENTAF. "After going through a series of security checks to receive an area access badge, I was tagged with an escort officer to help me get where I was going and to bring me up to speed on why I was there and what I would be doing." Tollini's escort was Major John Turk, with whom he would establish a close working relationship over the course of the air campaign. "Turk was much more than merely an 'escort' officer," recalled Tollini. "He was part of the CENTAF combat planning staff…[and] he could probably sense my awkwardness, with the enormous number of high-ranking officers floating around the place." Indeed, Rick Tollini was the only captain entering a room filled with colonels and generals.

"Good luck!" said Turk. "And watch out for Buster."

Tollini had no idea who "Buster" was, but the casual warning was enough to pique his interest. "I was not really sure what he [Turk] meant or why he felt the need to tell me that...but I would soon find out."

Looking around the room, Tollini quickly spotted another F-15 pilot, Lieutenant Colonel Dennis "Denny" Kremble from the 1st Fighter Wing at Langley. "I did not know Denny previously, but I recognized his wing patch on his shoulder, which told me right away he was an Eagle pilot. I quickly latched on to him so at least I had some common ground with somebody in the room, because I was the only captain in this obviously very important meeting." From among the sea of colonels and generals, there were only a handful of majors, all of whom seemed to be aids to the senior officers. "I thought surely Colonel Parsons had made a mistake," said Tollini, "or misunderstood his orders, and it was really supposed to be him at this meeting and not me." Regardless, Rick Tollini was now in the hot seat, representing the 58th Fighter Squadron at CENTAF Headquarters.

"With a rustling of officers and staff, and a quick scramble to seats," he continued, "the meeting was about to start as the 'star' of the show arrived"—Brigadier General Buster C. Glosson, the CENTAF Plans Director, better known as "Buster." Tollini soon realized that this was the man Turk had warned him about. But Tollini's initial impressions of Buster Glosson belied the warnings that Turk had given him. "Buster was smiling and seemed in a good mood," said Tollini, "and he appeared happy to be presiding over this obviously important meeting." General Glosson then began the meeting by outlining the initial plan for the air campaign against Iraq. At this point, Desert Shield was still a deterrent "show of force" mission; but the Iraqis had yet to respond to any diplomatic pressure. Thus, CENTAF wanted an operational plan for a full air campaign in the likely event that Saddam failed to withdraw from Kuwait.

As Tollini listened to the opening remarks, he felt that the entire scene was reminiscent of something from a World War II-era Hollywood picture. "If you can picture an old World War II movie," he said, "somewhere in an Allied bomber command operations center with a huge map that is unveiled to present 'Objective: Berlin'... it felt pretty much like that. A large covered board had been placed at the far end of the conference table, and as a staff officer removed the butcher paper layer it revealed an extensive map of Iraq." The large briefing map was riddled with symbols representing targets, aerial patrol sectors, and the disposition of comparative forces. "The briefer started into a synopsis of all the targets, taskings, and Allied air assets," Tollini continued. "The initial start to operations was intended to be a surprise attack in the middle of the night by a combination of land-attack cruise missiles and our new F-117 stealth fighters, taking out the Iraqis' main command-and-control (C2) radars and command centers to degrade their initial defensive air response. From there, our F-15C Eagles would spread out across the width of central and western Iraq and would perform a pure air superiority fighter sweep."

This meant that the 58th, along with the other F-15C squadrons, would patrol the skies, ready to pick off any Iraqi fighters that survived the initial bombardment. While running interference and shooting down Iraqi bandits, a continuous stream of bomber and attack aircraft would descend into Iraqi airspace, destroying all priority ground targets identified by CENTAF. Known as "strike packages," these ground attack missions would be accompanied by fighter escort and sweep protection flown by F-14s and F-15s. "It was impressive," recalled Tollini, "and I was pretty excited by what I was hearing and seeing...and this was just Day 1 of the operation that was being briefed." In fact, the size and scope of the mission seemed comparable to the Red Flag and Cope Thunder training maneuvers he had done for years. "There was nothing on the board that was much different than what I had been doing for so long now," he said.

"Once the brief was over, our job was to look over our tasking, figure out if there were any glaring issues or limitations to prevent our units from being able to perform our missions, and then to coordinate with any other unit representatives present to start the ball rolling on the long-range planning for this air campaign." Granted, it was only the "first draft" of the air war plan; Tollini knew that the plan would inevitably change as more coalition air units arrived in theater. "Denny and I set about divvying up the F-15 OCA [Offensive Counter Air] and DCA taskings." Unlike DCA missions, OCA represents an active and aggressive suppression of the enemy's air power. OCA missions include ground attack operations against enemy airfields and Combat Air Patrols (CAPs) with the purpose of gaining air superiority over a given area.

"The easiest thing to do," said Tollini, "was divide up most missions geographically." The 58th Fighter Squadron was at Tabuk in the west, and the 1st Fighter Wing squadrons were at Dhahran on the far east side of Saudi Arabia near Bahrain. "We pretty much ran a line straight from Baghdad…due south to the Saudi border, with the intent that the 58th would own any DCA CAPs and OCA strike missions west of that line." Meanwhile, the two squadrons from the 1st Fighter Wing would take any missions that fell east of that line. Shortly before the air war started, the F-15Cs from Bitburg Air Base, Germany also arrived in-theater. "We would split the difference and delegate a central corridor along that same line to the boys from Bitburg."

Determining these areas of responsibility, however, was the easy part. The challenge for Tollini was figuring out whether the 58th had the resources to accomplish their mission. "I knew from first glance that the sortie generation requirement (how many F-15s we could get into the air at any given time) was going to be a challenge and I would probably need more time and planning to make sure it could be done. But for now, it did not seem impossible."

It didn't take long, however, for Tollini to notice a problem that could wreck the entire mission. "There appeared to be a gap," he said, "in how many air-refueling tankers were tasked and how many external fuel tanks (bags) we would have available for flight operations." The KC-135 Stratotanker would be the coalition's workhorse for aerial refueling. As of yet, there weren't enough tankers in-theater, but CENTAF knew that more were on the way. The bigger issue that no one had seemed to notice, however, was the lack of external fuel tanks for the F-15s. "Just as in World War II," he said, "the advent of external drop tanks had extended the range and endurance of fighters such as the P-51 and P-47 over Europe and the Pacific; modern fighters would rely on them for the same reason. In peacetime training we rarely ever carried more than one or two 'bags,' as the external tanks were also known. If we did carry the maximum three-bag configuration, it was usually just for a long-range deployment trip from one base to another."

For most of their anticipated missions in Desert Storm, however, the F-15s would need to fly with all three tanks in order to meet their distance requirements. "This was fine," Tollini continued, "but we did not want to enter into any maneuvering fights or engagements with all that extra fuel and drag from the drop tanks. That is why they call them 'drop tanks.' The plan was that once we were committed to an engagement, we would immediately 'punch off' (drop) some or all of our external tanks."

The problem, however, was that the 58th had no additional drop tanks.

Indeed, their only drop tanks were the ones they had

flown with during the transatlantic flight from Eglin. As the conference started wrapping up, Buster Glosson re-entered the room.

"OK, fellas," he beamed. "You've seen the plan, and you've had time to look it over. I need to know today if anybody cannot accomplish their tasking."

From there, each unit representative went one-by-one, clockwise around the table giving his confirmation that their unit was up to the task.

"Yes sir."

"No problems here, Sir."

"Can-do, Sir."

When he got to Rick Tollini, the mood abruptly changed. Tollini remembered Turk's warning of Buster's fiery temper, and now he was about to see it on full display.

"Sir, we have a problem," Tollini began, "and it looks like we can't do our tasking."

The smile quickly disappeared from Buster's face.

"WHAT?" he barked. "What do you mean you can't do your missions? Why NOT?"

Tollini could almost feel the temperature rising.

"Well, Sir," said Tollini, "we should actually be able to do all of our initial missions with no problem, but we don't have any extra drop tanks."

Buster's stern countenance slowly changed to a look of genuine concern.

"We have enough tanks for our initial tasking," he continued, "but the first time we engage any Iraqi fighters we are going to drop our bags."

Buster nodded in agreement.

"So, when we get back to base, we won't have those tanks

anymore. We need extra drop tanks to be able to do the follow-on missions. That's the problem."

Buster's demeanor changed again...but not for the better.

"As he continued to face my way," Tollini recalled, "the look of 'interest' turned into a hard stare ... and then his face started turning red." The other officers in the room began to recoil, anticipating the general to erupt at any moment. "I began to sink slowly back into my chair hoping maybe I could just disappear." But just when he thought the general was going to explode, Buster turned to the staff colonel on his immediate left and bellowed:

"YOU GET THIS YOUNG MAN HIS DROP TANKS, YOU GOT THAT?"

"Wow!," Tollini thought to himself, "a last-second reprieve from the gallows."

He never learned the identity of the ill-fated colonel, but Tollini was glad not to have been on the business end of Buster's tirade. In fact, Tollini recalled there was an audible sigh of relief from the entire room as Buster finished his tirade and ended the conference.

Within a few hours, Rick Tollini was on his way back to Tabuk with the initial operations plan for the air war. Before he left the conference, however, he was told to keep the information "close hold"—meaning that he could only share the details with Rick Parsons and Bill Thiel. "I had a lot of work to do," he said, "and for now I would be doing it entirely on my own."

While settling into their daily rhythm at Tabuk, the 58th Fighter Squadron began to fly training sorties with the US Navy and the RSAF. JB Kelk recalled that those first few weeks in Saudi Arabia were spent learning the terrain, topography and developing contingencies for if and when the Iraqis descended into Saudi airspace. "The good news was that we were about 300 miles from the border," he said, which gave them some buffer time and enough of an early warning should the Iraqis fly into Saudi Arabia.

Still, the Americans' presence at Tabuk necessitated close cooperation with the Saudis. "We would sometimes fly against the Saudis in their F-5s," said ET Murphy. These mock dogfights would take place up and down the Arabian Peninsula, pitting F-15s against the Saudi F-5s in scenarios similar to what they'd see in combat against the IQAF. However, much to the chagrin of the RSAF, the Saudi pilots often struggled to keep pace with their American counterparts. After a while (and perhaps to save face), the RSAF began placing so many restrictions on the American fliers that the training value was quickly lost. "We tried to avoid working with them as time went on," Murphy continued.

Mark Arriola added: "We also got to fly against some Kuwaiti F1s that had managed to escape from Kuwait." Indeed, these refugee Kuwaiti pilots had fled to Saudi Arabia and were eager to join the coalition in its fight to take back the emirate. As it turned out, these F1 matchups were beneficial because the Iraqis had several Mirage F1s on hand—"and we needed to know what capabilities the French had put on those airplanes." But although a formidable fighter, the Mirage F1 was really no match for the F-15. Moreover, the Kuwaiti pilots' airmanship and dogfighting skills were as lackluster as most of their Arab counterparts. Their doctrinal reliance on GCI had hamstrung the pilots' ability to make independent decisions while in the air.

With little training value to be had from the RSAF or the Free Kuwaitis, the 58th Fighter Squadron turned its attention to the US naval air squadrons anchored in the Red Sea. "We established a liaison with the USS *Kennedy* and the *Saratoga*," said Chuck Magill. As a Marine aviator, he was grateful for the newfound relationship. In 1990, interoperability between naval and Air Force squadrons was practically nonexistent. Flying these practice sorties against one another would improve inter-service communication and facilitate an exchange of ideas while learning comparative capabilities. "The Air Force F-15 community is a strongly-opinionated group," Magill continued—implying that the F-15 community tended to see itself as the best of America's aviators. "But when you get shot off a carrier deck, go fly a mission, and then come back for a carrier landing at night in bad weather, you gain a whole new appreciation for that," said Magill. "In the Air Force, all you have to do is find a 12,000-foot runway and land. It's not that hard. But the choreography on the carrier deck is just extraordinary. Almost everyone in the squadron spent some time with the Navy, up in the CIC [control tower] watching landings with Tomcats, A-6s, A-7s, and Hornets. They came back with a new appreciation for the Navy, which I was very grateful for."

ET Murphy was one such pilot with a newfound appreciation for his seafaring comrades. "The Navy wanted to practice sending big strike packages against the ranges near our base," he said. For the upcoming air war, the Navy anticipated sending in waves of ground attack aircraft, accompanied by F-14 Tomcats and F/A-18 Hornets for fighter sweep and escort missions. During these joint training missions with the 58th Fighter Squadron, Murphy recalled that the Navy sent messages "tasking a four-ship of our Eagles to defend the ranges." As Murphy described it: "That was the cat's meow because we got to practice radar work and four-ship employment. Those Navy strikes combined air-to-air escorts and bombers trying to hit us, so we never knew what to expect. It was really good training for a mass raid. The training high point was working with the Navy; those guys were really good."

Sheepishly, however, Chuck Magill admitted that the F-14 Tomcat, the veritable "crown jewel" of the Navy's carrier fleet, underperformed when it was pitted against the F-15 Eagle. "The F-14 was a *terrible* plane for overland operations," he said. "With their pulse radar, they could hardly see anything. We'd roll right over them." As Magill recalled, the F-14 had been optimized for seaborne operations, shooting down aggressor aircraft within hundreds of miles of the carrier group—"the plane wasn't suited for anything over land."

Aside from their Saudi hosts, the Americans were also sharing the Tabuk Air Base with a British Tornado squadron. But whereas the Americans were instructed to be sensitive to Arab culture, "the Brits acted like Brits," said Chuck Magill. "They played rugby in shorts"—clothing that was forbidden by Saudi law. "And whenever the Saudis drove by to see the spectacle," he continued, "the Brits would holler: 'We're Number One!'" According to Mark Arriola: "The Brits basically said to the Saudi government: 'F*ck you guys, we conquered this country once before, we'll do it again. So we're going to do whatever we want.'"

Their actions certainly matched their attitude.

"They built their own tent city at Tabuk," said Arriola. "They had booze going and they'd walk around with their shirts off"—two more violations of Saudi law.

Aside from their bombastic flippancies, Magill admitted that these RAF pilots were among the best in the world, and certainly the most daring. "I wouldn't climb into a British Tornado for anything on the planet," he chuckled. "They are the craziest aviators, but also *very* skilled. For these Tornado pilots, flying 50 feet above the deck through the mountains was no problem at all."

As the coalition grew, a few pilots in the 58th took opportunities to hop aboard the so-called "Camel Express."

As Chuck Magill recalled: "We'd hop on these American C-130s and go to places like Dharan and Abu Dhabi"— where they would meet incoming wing commanders from stateside bases who were just arriving into theater. During these meetings, Magill and Tollini would develop interoperability and contingency plans for working alongside these newcomer units once the air war began.

Taken together, their DCA patrols, HVAA escorts, and joint training missions put the squadron on a 24-hour operations cycle, rotating pilots on and off the stream of continuously flying aircraft. "We quickly settled into a four-day rotating schedule," said ET Murphy. "We'd fly during the day, then fly at night, then pull alert, and have the fourth day off." Bill Theil added: "We had four aircraft on alert at all times: two aircraft on a five-minute alert; two aircraft on a fifteen-minute alert." Daytime missions typically lasted eight hours with the night missions launching after midnight. "That change kind of screws up your circadian rhythm, so you'd spend the second day trying to get some rest and eat," said Murphy. "We never got used to that. The alert days were spent with four guys ready to launch in five minutes from a little shack with beds, a TV, a VCR, a bathroom, and a kitchen."

But even during their rest cycles, the pilots refused to stay idle. "In a fighter squadron," said Bruce Till, "you're always in training mode. When you get back from a sortie, you're studying tactics for the rest of the day—red tactics [enemy], blue tactics [friendly], and anything to get yourself ready for the next mission; just like we did at home." Mark Arriola, meanwhile, as one of the most junior pilots on the deployment, took it as an opportunity to level-up his flight ratings. With all the mission cycles, Mark remembered that: "I got an opportunity to do my 'flight lead' upgrade training." After a certain number of training hours, a junior pilot could upgrade to "flight lead" qualification, meaning that he could lead and maneuver a two or four-ship formation.

But to keep the planes operational for their continuing missions, Matos and his maintenance crews had to work around the clock. Before and after every mission, Matos, McGirr, and several ground crewmen would walk the flight line and runways, looking for any debris or foreign objects. The runway had to be clear of even the smallest debris, lest it bounce into an air intake or afterburner. Even the smallest metal shard or unassuming rock could disrupt the F-15's engine manifold if it bounced up from the runway.

"The F-15 is a fragile, fragile piece of equipment," said Matos. "Everything on the plane has to work just right…it has to be properly serviced or it won't fly"—or, if it did fly, it could suffer an in-flight malfunction that would down the plane or impact the pilot's mission capabilities. "The crew chiefs always came in the morning," Matos continued. "Each F-15 had a dedicated crew chief; and he would inspect each of the support sections' toolboxes. Because each tool box was different—engines, hydraulics, avionics—they were checked against their own accountability lists. God help you if you lost a tool!" The crew chief would then act as a final quality control manager, checking the vital functions of the plane before it was deemed airworthy.

But, as Todd McGirr noted: "The average sortie length had quadrupled our run time for pumps, generators, and basic equipment inside the airplane." Indeed, the cyclic eight-hour missions had begun taking their toll on the F-15s' internal hardware. "Because of the number of hours we were building up, we encountered an immediate problem with parts availability," said McGirr. Given the magnitude of Desert Shield, Air Force leaders were struggling to find enough spare parts to accommodate the long-term mission. "So, we had to change our thinking when it came to spare parts."

Luckily, the 58th Fighter Squadron had an advocate in their supply officer. "We had this young supply officer," said Matos, "Captain Dave Underwood. And this guy was a superstar. He did anything to get us spare parts." In fact, the maintenance team owed much of their success to Captain Underwood's resourcefulness. As Chief Matos concluded: "We can fix what we can, as fast as we can; but if we don't have the parts, we're not going anywhere."

Still, the 58th was not immune to improvising. "We were having problems with common hardware," said Todd McGirr. "Connector plugs, motors, things like that. So, we started doing things like hard-wiring starters, which is illegal as hell, but you don't have a choice." These field-expedient repairs, however, soon gave way to the real hardware. Thanks to the resourcefulness of Captain Underwood and the organizational supervision of Chief Matos, the 58th never had to go too long without the components it needed to maintain a high readiness rate.

In between their missions, the pilots found a number of ways to keep themselves occupied. "We got into pretty good shape," said JB Kelk. "They had a really nice gym on the base with an Olympic-size swimming pool." Mark Arriola was likewise fascinated by the fitness amenities. "It was just a spectacular facility," he recalled. "And it was run by Filipino immigrants." Like many of the oil-producing Gulf States, the Saudis often delegated their menial and clerical work to third-party immigrants.

The pilots also had opportunities to venture into downtown Tabuk, although the Saudi nightlife was virtually non-existent. In fact, being in Saudi Arabia was a culture shock for many in the 58th. "Saudi Arabia was a strange country," said Rick Tollini. "I don't mean that necessarily in a bad way, but just that it felt 'strange' being there. I had been in a lot of foreign countries, but this was the first time I had felt like such a 'foreigner,' like I did not belong there. The people were nice enough, and most of us even made friends with many of the Saudi pilots. But it just always felt like there was some kind of barrier, as if we were the houseguests that had impolitely overstayed our visit...I felt they probably really preferred it if we would leave, as soon as possible. And, frankly, I felt the same way."

Although they were free to go downtown, the American fliers still had to be mindful that they were in a foreign country. Iraqi spies could be lingering and, of course, the Americans had to be mindful of Sharia law. In the Tabuk town square, for instance, public floggings and executions were carried out on a daily basis. "We were always armed whenever we went downtown," said Mark Arriola. "We carried our sidearms." Indeed, with memories of Panama still fresh in their minds, commanders were leery of rogue governments (even those who were considered "allies") taking American servicemen hostage, much like Noriega had done in 1989. "And we never went downtown by ourselves," Arriola continued. "We always went with a pack of guys."

And although they were guests of a decidedly Islamic country, they still found pieces of Western culture on the streets of Tabuk. "They had Kentucky Fried Chicken, McDonald's, and even a Dairy Queen," said Arriola. However, he questioned the legitimacy of what the Saudis called "chicken" or "beef." Indeed, these entrees bore little resemblance to the fast food he had seen in the West.

"But once Desert Storm kicked off, we were restricted to the base."

It was just as well; because venturing into Tabuk would often draw negative attention from the Saudi Religious Police. As the name implied, their mission was to enforce the metrics of Islamic piety on the local population. And they would never pass up the opportunity to shake down a visiting foreigner.

One day, Bruce Till and Chuck Magill were nearly arrested by the Saudi Religious Police. Chuck and Bruce were out taking pictures, when suddenly they were cornered by a squad of rogue police officers. "They kept yelling at us and pointing to our cameras."

The pilots were dumbfounded.

They hadn't been doing anything wrong nor had they taken photographs of any forbidden sites. But neither man was prepared to surrender his camera.

Finally, one of the religious cops intimated that he wanted their film.

Not wanting to risk landing in a Saudi jail, both men reluctantly surrendered their cameras' film. It was ironic— the only "police brutality" they had witnessed came from the Saudi Religious Police who, quite frankly, had a reputation for causing trouble and inventing problems where none existed. The civil law enforcement police, however, were friendly towards Americans. "They realized we were on a mission and that we were there to help," said Bruce Till. "But the Religious Police were on a mission, too. They were out to prove that they could push us around. But they figured out pretty quickly that we weren't going to put up with that."

Amidst these occasional run-ins with the Saudi gestapo, American pilots found refuge in the local United States Military Training Mission (USMTM).[5] As Rick Tollini described it, the USMTM was a "high-walled, secure compound" away from the airbase, situated in the town of

---

[5] Pronounced "you-suh-mitt-um"

Tabuk proper. "There were many USMTMs across the Middle East and in other countries," he said, "and they were where US military foreign liaison personnel lived in-country to assist our allies with training and operations." Although the Tabuk airbase was a nice facility, it paled in comparison to the USMTM. Their liaison personnel lived in nice apartments, had access to a lovely swimming pool, and enjoyed a fully-stocked bar. "There was supposed to be no alcohol allowed on base while we were in-country," said Tollini, "but the USMTMs were different. They were a little piece of 'America' and had immunity from local laws and customs."

The USMTM at Tabuk was commanded by Air Force Major Ken "Crash" McKean. "He welcomed us with open arms," said Mark Arriola. "We could go there to do laundry and catch up on CNN...just to see what the world was doing." Coincidentally, McKean was also an F-15 pilot and occasionally flew sorties alongside the 58th during their time in Saudi Arabia. Although an F-15 pilot by trade, his role as the USMTM commander made him an attaché to the Royal Saudi Air Force, wherein he had logged several hours aboard an F-5 Tiger.

The alcohol oasis at the USMTM, however, quickly dried up in the wake of General H. Norman Schwarzkopf's issuance of General Order #1. The order mandated that no American servicemen were permitted to drink alcohol within the Kingdom of Saud. "This was hopefully to show 'solidarity' with our Saudi hosts," said Rick Tollini, "and not insult their cultural sensibilities."

But many thought that General Order #1 was excessive.

"Even most Saudis I met who heard about this no-drinking order thought it was crazy," Tollini continued. "They really didn't care if we drank as long as we behaved."

Despite the oppressive yoke of General Order #1, a few

industrious airmen found ways to smuggle fine spirits into theater. "One of the most ingenious," said Tollini, "was when one of our pilots received a huge stuffed animal in the mail from his old college roommate. We all looked at him like he must've had a really strange relationship with his roommate. What fighter pilot would want to receive a cute stuffed doggie? But when he accidently dropped the gift, it made a tinkling sound. That poor stuffed animal did not last another 10 seconds as it was ripped open and out spilled about 30 airline booze miniatures. We tried to make those last as long as possible."

Another pilot recalled receiving a box of chocolate chip cookies from his brother in the States. This cookie box, however, was carefully crafted to conceal an even bigger surprise waiting inside: a bottle of liquor. This same pilot had a resourceful fiancée who likewise mailed him a bottle of scotch. "Of course, that bottle never left my room," he chuckled, "but my roommate and I put a pretty big dent in it!"

Doc Cornum was another surprising source of illegal alcohol. "His wife Rhonda was stationed in Bahrain," said Tollini, "where it was possible to purchase alcohol. Normally, if we were sitting around the USMTM pool, Doc Cornum would come around with an IV bag that he had filled with vodka while he was in Bahrain." In between these poolside libations, however, Tollini admitted that: "we would find some other kind of chemical to put in our system; for most of us that would be caffeine and nicotine."

As the days droned on, many pilots kept themselves busy by playing cards, writing letters, listening to their Walkmans, or trying to level-up on whatever Nintendo Gameboy cartridges they had found. Rick Tollini, for example, had become quite adept at playing *Super Mario Land*. "For me, it was not important to complete the game to the final finish," he said, "but rather just how many 'lives' I could retain at the end of play."

Other pilots preferred simply to rest. "The days off were spent catching up on eating and sleeping," said Tony Murphy. "I remember listening to Radio Free America," added Chuck Magill, "which was the only English-language radio station you could get; everything else was in a foreign language." Magill, however, was able to buy a stereo at one of the local businesses in Tabuk, which came in handy during their hours of crew rest. Now, instead of relying on their battery-powered Walkmans, the fliers could enjoy their cassette tapes in stereo sound. "We also had to get used to the time change," Magill continued. "It was about 12-13 hours different." Indeed, even the world's best pilots couldn't shake the effects of jet lag.

Although writing and receiving letters was their only contact with the outside world, it was often painful because it reminded them of life beyond Tabuk. Still, the 58th Fighter Squadron was touched by the random letters they received from schoolchildren, offering words of encouragement and the unshakable optimism of grade-school youth. These sentiments were also reflected in the many care packages they received. During the early days of Desert Shield, care packages addressed to "Any Serviceman" flowed into Saudi Arabia by the thousands. Filled to capacity with baked goods, toiletries, and magazines, these packages came from families and civic organizations across the US. From the content and quantity of these packages, it seemed as though Americans collectively felt bad for how they had treated their Vietnam veterans, and were determined to make up for it. The packages that arrived in Tabuk, especially those containing muffins and brownies, brightened the otherwise dull routines of the desert air base. "The support we received was just unbelievable," said

Kelk.

US servicemen were often told: "If you don't mess with the wildlife, it won't mess with you." Still, every man in the 58th had run-ins with the local desert fauna. "When the sun went down, the flies left and the mosquitoes showed up," said Murphy. "A truck came by to fog the place, which concerned us because we'd choke on that stuff. You'd run into your room to get away from the truck but so would the mosquitoes. They were so bad that I could hear them through the earplugs at night." On other occasions, the pilots and ground crews had close encounters with snakes, scorpions, and the dreaded camel spiders.

Mark Arriola, for example, recalled one evening when he and a few other pilots were sitting quietly outside the alert hut. "Then all of a sudden, we start hearing this sound: *Fssst…plop! Fssst…plop!*" Deducing that the noise had come from the nearest alert hangar, Mark and his friends were shocked to see a family of vipers slithering out from a hole in the upper wall, then falling 10-12 feet to the ground before slithering off.

"It was something right out of Indiana Jones," he said with a chuckle.

"And the next thing I knew, there were three or four maintenance guys trying to capture one of these snakes." The maintenance crews succeeded in capturing one elusive viper while, simultaneously, a few of the avionics technicians wrangled a camel spider. The enlisted airmen then set up an impromptu fighting ring, pitting the snake against the camel spider. As a crowd gathered around the impromptu cockfight, some of the spectators began taking bets.

The outcome, however, was rather shocking.

"That camel spider killed the snake within seconds!" said Mark.

The sight literally made him sick to his stomach, but many of the enlisted onlookers were cheering. "The difference, I think, between the 'enlisted mindset' and the 'officer mindset' is that I'm sure we would have thought of it, but we never would have acted on it…whereas these guys were just bored silly and they were looking for something to do." However, when news of the reptilian cockfights reached Bill Thiel and Rick Parsons, they immediately quashed it. There forward, every man in the 58th was forbidden from wrangling *any* of the local wildlife.

Coincidentally, however, the topography and terrain of northwestern Saudi Arabia was remarkably similar to what they had seen during the annual Red Flag exercises at Nellis Air Force Base in Nevada. As such, the pilots were already accustomed to operating in a high desert environment. But although protected by an enclosed canopy (and a pressurized cockpit), a pilot still had to maintain proper hydration before and after every mission. "We were *all* drinking bottled water," said JB Kelk. "Every day, a C-130 came in and delivered palettes of water bottles." For Chief Matos and the maintenance crews, however, the bigger problem was the fine dust and sand. "It was getting into the umbilical cords for the missiles,"—the cleaning of which added several more hours of maintenance.

As summer turned to fall, Rick Tollini stayed busy reviewing the squadron's anticipated missions for the upcoming air war. If and when hostilities came, Tollini wanted to ensure that the 58th was ready to take on the IQAF. "Over the next several months" he said, "I would often walk from our operations building all the way down the flight line to our intelligence center," where he would occupy a secure room and go over the mission requirements in solitude. "I had a yellow legal pad and I came up with a way to start managing pilots and airplanes." The 58th Fighter Squadron had deployed to Tabuk with twenty-four F-15s and thirty pilots. This created a ratio of 1.25 pilots per jet. Although this was a normal pilot-to-plane ratio for peacetime training, Tollini soon discovered that it would be woefully inadequate for continuous combat operations.

"My first step in task planning," he said, "was to create dedicated 4-ship pairings for the pilots," meaning that he would match up a selection of designated flight leads and wingmen. His intent was to have each man of the four-ship pairing stay together throughout the air war. "The advantage of the pairings," he continued, "was that we would be so familiar with each other within each flight that it would eliminate the need to constantly brief and debrief missions. We would understand each other's strengths and weaknesses and know what to expect of each other in certain situations." Moreover, these consistent four-ship pairings facilitated easier scheduling. "I gave each pilot an alphanumeric number that signified what 4-ship he was in and the position he could fly in that 4-ship. I would use these alphanumeric designations for the pilots and the jets, and go through the air tasking order to try to get the most efficient use out of each."

Tollini soon discovered that although he had enough F-15s, he kept running out of pilots to fulfill the sortie generation requirements. "The planners [in Riyadh] were relying on their peacetime training and exercise experience," he said, "where the emphasis was always to generate as many sorties as possible." Under these conditions, the pilots and jets would have a quick turnaround—"refuel, rearm, and ready for the next mission"—with a steady stream of pilots replacing those who were going into their rest cycle. "The only problem," said Tollini, "is that peacetime training and exercises normally only ran on an 8–12-hour flying window." Desert Storm, however, was going to be an around-the-clock operation.

"The peacetime planning did not work."

Tollini also noticed that CENTAF's mandated two-hour DCA missions were too short; they hadn't factored in the travel time to and from the assigned patrol sectors. Taken together, the mission parameters, combined with briefings, debriefings, etc., would put the pilots on a 14–16-hour schedule. "This might be OK for maybe a day or two," he noted, "but after that our pilots would be run into the ground with fatigue."

Come what may, the DCA missions had to be longer.

"Once I had that epiphany," he said, "the solutions became very clear." If he could convince Riyadh to authorize six-hour missions, it would reduce the sortie generation requirements. Each jet would fly only twice during a 24-hour period, providing more downtime for maintenance and facilitating longer crew rests.

As it turned out, Tollini had no problem convincing Riyadh to authorize the six-hour sorties. Moreover, Chief Matos and the maintenance teams were more than ready to accommodate the projected mission timelines. The squadron had twenty-four F-15s, and from those twenty-four, Tollini asked the maintenance handlers if they could provide at least twenty total "frontlines"—meaning twenty F-15s ready to fly at any given moment. That was a very high percentage even for peacetime flying, but Matos, McGirr, and the maintenance crews assured Tollini that it could be done.

Thus, with twenty available jets, the squadron could provide eight F-15s for 24-hour DCA coverage with one four-ship flight on patrol the entire time. "While four Eagles were on CAP [Combat Air Patrol], our maintainers would have 3–4 hours to get the next 4-ship ready." Four other F-15s, meanwhile, would remain on standby in a Quick Reaction Alert (QRA) posture. These QRA jets also provided a critical backfill for any DCA aircraft that had to "return early for maintenance or reload," said Rick Tollini, "or to act as maintenance spare aircraft for the OCA mission requirements." But there was still a manpower problem—"it was obvious we didn't have enough pilots." Indeed, to accommodate the anticipated mission parameters, the squadron would need at least 36 pilots. "We only had 30."

Tollini asked Thiel if they could bring in more pilots from Eglin. Sadly, Bill's hands were tied. The US Air Force already had tens of thousands of personnel in theater, and CENTAF refused to listen to the growing chorus of stateside airmen who were begging for deployments.

"In our case though," Rick said, "we really needed the extra pilots."

Unable to secure extra pilots, Tollini decided to change the 24-hour mission cycle to an 18-hour cycle. "If we had about 40 sorties every 24 hours, then in an 18-hr window we would have about 30 sorties. That's exactly how many pilots we had." Still, the scheduling would be tight. And each pilot would have an earlier "hit time" for every successive mission. For example, if a pilot flew the 12:00–6:00 PM mission on Day 1 of the air war, his next mission on Day 2 would start six hours earlier (flying from 6:00 AM –12:00 PM), and so forth. "Imagine this," said Tollini: "You wake up at 6 AM, work from 8 AM to 5 PM, get to sleep as soon as you can, and then wake up at midnight, and then start the cycle again six hours earlier each day. It was crazy, but we had to do it."

Moreover, it violated the 12-hour peacetime crew-rest requirements.

"We were going to be lucky to get 4–5 hours of sleep every night," he added, "not to mention the constantly changing biorhythm of getting up six hours earlier each day. But this wasn't going to be 'peacetime.' This was going to be combat."

When Bill Thiel approved Rick Tollini's plan, Thiel predicted that coalition forces would gain air superiority within the first two weeks of combat, and that the squadron's operational tempo would decrease thereafter. "He was right about the first part," said Tollini, "but not the second." Indeed, their op tempo would increase *exponentially* during the second month of the air war. Whether flying HVAA or pre-strike fighter sweeps, "everybody wanted Eagles on their wings, protecting them."

On November 9, 1990, President Bush announced that the US VII Corps and additional air assets in Europe would deploy to Saudi Arabia. By now, it had become increasingly clear that the Iraqis would not respond to a diplomatic solution. These additional forces demonstrated the President's resolve that the occupation of Kuwait would be reversed by force if necessary. This deployment would raise the number of US forces in the Persian Gulf to more than 400,000 by the end of the year. That Thanksgiving, President Bush flew to Saudi Arabia to enjoy a holiday feast with the frontline troops; and the 58th Fighter Squadron had the honor of escorting Air Force One into Saudi airspace. One week later, the UN Security Council passed Resolution 678. The resolution, for what it was worth, gave Saddam Hussein a deadline of January 15 to withdraw his forces, or face military action. Still, the Iraqi dictator showed no signs of backing down.

Christmas 1990 was as enjoyable of a celebration as one could have in Saudi Arabia. Despite the overbearing presence of Sharia law, the Americans were allowed to have a private service on Christmas eve. Jewish servicemen, however, weren't so lucky. They had to be flown out to shipboard synagogues aboard American carriers in the Gulf. The 58th Fighter Squadron, meanwhile, captured its own yuletide celebration on a VHS camcorder. As a collective gift for their families back home, the squadron made a video highlighting their daily routines at Tabuk. "The spouses and kids back home got to see our general operating environment," said Rico Rodriguez. "They got to see our gym, the pool, the flight line, and things like that." And each member of the squadron had enough camera time to wish his family a Merry Christmas. It was a touching gift for the families of the deployed airmen.

Meanwhile, back on the home front, the families of the 58th did their best to support each other. ET Murphy's wife, Christine, remembered that: "Our squadron's 'wives support system' worked really well since there were many women in the same situation, many of them with children. We got frustrated at the lack of information, of course. I guess families should never know everything, but there was so much misinformation in the rumor mill that it was nearly impossible to cut through it and figure out the truth. There were rumors like: We couldn't use stamps with the American flag on them because the Saudis wouldn't allow it; the guys would be home for Thanksgiving; they'll be home for Christmas...you just never knew what to believe. The leaders in the squadron did try really hard to give us the information they had."

To that end, the families found an advocate in Colonel Rich "Tuna" Hardy, Director of Operations (DO) for the 33d Fighter Wing. Hardy himself was a certified "MiG killer," having downed a North Vietnamese MiG-21 in combat over Southeast Asia. As the DO, he had become the Wing's "rear detachment commander" for the duration of Colonel Parsons' absence. In his newfound role, Hardy took great strides to keep the Wing spouses and children updated on the happenings of their loved ones in the Gulf.

Meanwhile, public support from the local community was tremendous. "They talked on the radio and TV, businesses put supportive words on their signs, and folks were willing to help any family that needed it," said Christine Murphy. "Friends would have groups of wives over for dinner to keep their minds on something besides war."

But as the holiday season came and went, the pilots of the 58th began to ponder what they'd be facing in the upcoming months. Indeed, by the middle of December it had been four and a half months since Iraq invaded Kuwait. No progress had been made on the diplomatic front and the Butcher of Baghdad was now less than one month away from his January 15 deadline.

Rick Tollini, meanwhile, by virtue of his position as the Weapons Officer (and his close proximity to the CENTAF planning cells), was the only man in the squadron with a real-time knowledge of the burgeoning war plans. By late December 1990, Tonic allowed him to brief the finalized plan covering the squadron's anticipated operations for the first three days of the air war. The proviso, however, was that Tollini could only brief the designated mission commanders.

"I already had them picked out," he said.

Now, he could finally share the plan he had worked so meticulously to build—four-ship formations; 18-hour mission cycles; and designated crew rosters for every sortie. I had already scheduled every single sortie and pilot for the three-day ATO," he said. "I knew whom I wanted to lead and fly in each and every mission." The mission commanders would be: Tollini himself; Jon "JB" Kelk; Chuck "Sly" Magill; Rory "Hoser" Draeger; and Rob "Cheese" Graeter. "These were all the key players," said Tollini, "who would lead the critical missions in the first three days of Operation Desert Storm."

Each mission commander held the rank of captain, meaning they were all "junior officers" with approximately

6-8 years of service. "My judgement was (and still is) that generally the most proficient and capable combat leaders are the captains," said Tollini. After all, the captains and senior lieutenants did most of the flying. Majors and lieutenant colonels often had to divide their time between flying and the tedium of staff work. "Fortunately, I had a squadron commander [Bill Thiel] who agreed with me." Indeed, Tonic was more than willing to defer the tactical employment of the squadron's aircraft to the young captains. "I credit his wise determination on this issue as a key to our eventual outstanding success in aerial combat," said Rick Tollini.

After New Year's Day 1991, Tollini finally got permission to brief the entire squadron on the air campaign plan. "Pilots already knew what their 4-ship pairings were," he said, "and in this brief they would find out what missions they were tagged to perform." Some pilots would be flying OCA missions, while others would be on DCA patrol or QRA backfill missions. "The OCA teams had to be our very best 4-ships and mission commanders. Although there were a few young and inexperienced wingmen in some of these pairings, they were always surrounded by strong flight members. The DCA teams would not be expected to see as much action, and so for that reason I could pair some of the less-experienced flight members together." Still, every DCA mission had a strong flight leader to guide them along. Case in point was Captain Joe "Corn" Hruska. "He was by far one of our most talented young flight leads," Tollini recalled, "and I would have preferred to have Corn in the OCA lineups, but I gave him responsibility to fly with and watch over one of our squadron leaders. Corn's job was to keep him alive."

With the plan in place, and the parties fully briefed, the only question was when the air war would start. "We had been in Tabuk long enough and everybody wanted to go home." But by now, the pilots were saying: "The quickest way home is through Baghdad." Given that Saddam had a deadline of January 15, many pilots assumed that the air campaign would start the same day.

Rick Tollini, however, wasn't so sure.

"Just like the D-Day invasion," he said, "the date to start combat operations depended on the seasons and the phase of the moon. We wanted a near moonless night for the Tomahawks, F-117s, and other strike aircraft to do their work under the cover of almost total darkness. There were only so many of those days every month." Based on the lunar cycles, therefore, it seemed that the best launching dates would fall between January 16-19.

On the morning of January 15, 1991, the 58th Fighter Squadron awoke to the news that Saddam Hussein had reached his deadline, and had made no effort to withdraw from Kuwait. The next day, President Bush announced the start of the military campaign to eject the Iraqis from the war-torn emirate. "I was up flying," recalled JB Kelk. "I had the graveyard shift and I remember, after landing, I got the de-brief at around 7:00 AM on the 16th." He could tell by the look on Tonic Thiel's face that the air war was imminent.

"We're on," said Thiel.

Operation Desert Shield had just become Operation Desert Storm.

Pilots from the 58th Fighter Squadron prepare to deploy to Operation Desert Shield, August 1990.

Ground crews at Eglin Air Force Base perform their pre-flight checks and maintenance on the F-15Cs as the 58th prepares to deploy.

Personnel from the 58th Fighter Squadron line the runway to see their pilots depart for Southwest Asia.

The F-15Cs prepare to take flight from Eglin Air Force Base.

At the Tabuk Air Base, pilots take pause for a moment of levity. Clockwise from left to right: Robert "LA" Brooks; Scott "Papa" Maw; Mark "Nips" Arriola; and Chuck "Sly" Magill.

Mark Arriola and Scott Maw pose for the camera during the early days of Desert Shield, Tabuk Air Base.

Chuck Magill and Tony Murphy go "shirtless" while enjoying some downtime near the flight line at Tabuk. Although Saudi law prohibited men to go around shirtless (or wear shorts), the authorities typically ignored such practices so long as the Americans were confined to the base.

Mark Arriola (left) and a few of his comrades pose in front of an F-15 within a hardened shelter at Tabuk. The shelters belonged to the Royal Saudi Air Force (RSAF) and had been built to accommodate the smaller and leaner F-5 Tigers. As such, the aircraft shelters were so small that the F-15s barely had one foot of wing clearance on either side.

F-15s from the 58th Fighter Squadron conduct joint training maneuvers with some Saudi F-5 Tigers during Desert Shield. In the early days of their deployment, the 58th flew several training sorties alongside the RSAF and the few Kuwaiti Air Force jets that had managed to escape the invasion.

An F-15C from the 1st Fighter Wing (based at Langley AFB), sits in a revetment at its air base in Dharan. The 1st Fighter Wing worked closely with the 58th Fighter Squadron throughout Desert Shield and Desert Storm. Note the Patriot missile battery in the background. Patriot missiles had been stationed throughout the Kingdom to protect coalition forces from Iraqi Scuds.

A Kuwaiti A-4 Skyhawk and an American F-15 from the 1st Tactical Fighter Wing prior to a mission. Note the inscription "Free Kuwait" on the A-4's fuselage – indicating that the A-4 was part of the Kuwaiti military operating in exile.

As Desert Shield dragged on, the pilots of the 58th found a number of ways to keep themselves entertained. Here, a group of pilots pose atop an Air Force Security Police Humvee, brandishing the policemen's weapons. From left to right: Mark Arriola; Scott Maw; Robert Brooks; and Chuck Magill.

Captain Rhory Draeger. As the Weapons Officer of the neighboring 59th Fighter Squadron, Drager deployed with the 58th as a backfill when the pre-MQT pilots in the 58th were left behind at Eglin. Draeger had a solid reputation as one of the toughest and smartest fighter pilots in the 33d Fighter Wing. His comrades were genuinely shocked when he left active duty after the war. He did, however, remain in the Air National Guard. Tragically, Draeger was killed in an automobile accident in 1995.

Bruce "Roto" Till poses in front of his F-15. During Desert Shield, Till had a close encounter with an Iraqi Mirage F1 that inadvertently crossed the Saudi border. Unfortunately, the Iraqi F1 darted back across the border before Till could fire off a shot.

Bruce Till on the deck of the USS *John F. Kennedy*. Throughout Desert Shield, the 58th Fighter Squadron flew several training sorties with their US Navy counterparts, and kept a close liaison with the naval air squadrons throughout the air war.

Rick "Kluso" Tollini enjoying the daily news from his officer's quarters at Tabuk.

★ Capt. Rico Rodriguez ★

Cesar Rodriguez and one of his maintenance crewmen conduct their final preparations before a combat mission, January 1991. Rodriguez shot down two enemy planes during Desert Storm—a MiG-23 and a MiG-29. Eight years later, during the air war over Yugoslavia, Rodriguez shot down a third MiG-29 near the city of Pristina.

January 21, 1991. An F-15C from the 58th vectors away from its KC-135 Stratotanker after topping off on fuel.

Larry "Cherry" Pitts takes a self-portrait over Iraq.

Col. Rick N. Parsons

Colonel Rick Parsons, commander of the 33d Fighter Wing, prepares his plane for combat. A 1966 Air Force Academy graduate, Parsons flew several combat sorties over Vietnam and Iraq. Although he was the wing commander, he nevertheless deployed with the 58th Fighter Squadron, and was credited with multiple air-to-air victories. Parsons tragically passed away on May 25, 2021.

Tony "ET" Murphy returns to base after downing two Iraqi Su-22 fighter-bombers on February 7, 1991.

The remains of an Iraqi MiG-25 after being destroyed on the ground by a 2,000-pound laser-guided bomb. During Desert Storm, a good portion of the Iraqi Air Force was destroyed before it ever went airborne. Even more Iraqi planes were destroyed during the ensuing years as the US and its NATO partners enforced the Iraqi No-Fly Zones.

The fuselage of Colonel Rick Parsons's F-15C, decorated with the markings annotating his air-to-air kills in the skies over Iraq.

The pilots of the 58th Fighter Squadron pose atop an F-15C. The 58th earned the distinction of killing more enemy planes than any other Allied unit in Iraq. They also achieved the most double-kills, and were the first unit to down a MiG-29 in combat.

Chapter 4

A DAWN LIKE THUNDER

On January 17, at 2:38 AM, Baghdad time, the first wave of the coalition's air campaign destroyed Iraqi radar sites near the Saudi border. For the next five weeks, coalition air forces pounded away at key targets in Iraq and Kuwait, while clearing the skies of any Iraqi resistance. "I spent three days aboard the JFK [USS Kennedy] doing mission planning for the first night of the air war," said Kelk—deconflicting flight schedules and brokering deals to occupy different pieces of airspace. On the eve of Desert Storm, US Naval Aviation and their Air Force counterparts were jockeying to get in on the action. Each wanted to prove their mettle against the IQAF, but inter-service communication was hard because the Navy and Air Force operated on different systems, and very often with different procedures. "We didn't want to be in the air at the same time," said Kelk, "so we had to deconflict our efforts." As Kelk described it, each service would have their own respective airspaces and mission times. But as it turned out, the F-15s would take the lion's share of air-to-air victories during Desert Storm.

Saddam Hussein, for his part, had not been idle during the buildup to the air campaign. He had prepared his fighter-interceptor units at air bases including Al-Taqqadum, Al-Asad, Mudaysis, H-2, and H-3. Unlike the Iraqi Army, whose frontline formations were manned mostly by conscripts, the Iraqi Air Force had the best-trained and highest-quality personnel. With hostilities imminent, Saddam instructed his pilots to destroy the "infidels" who were about to descend onto Iraq.

Meanwhile, back in the States, ET Murphy's wife, Christine, learned about the air war in the same way most Air Force spouses did: CNN. "I got into the habit of eating near the TV because I hate to eat alone," she said. "Then news about the bombs going off in Baghdad came on with the CNN reporters saying they really didn't know what was going on. It was fascinating. At first, I thought the reporters blew it out of proportion and there wasn't much happening. Then, I flipped through all the channels to see if they agreed and finally realized the war had started. From that first news report on, I was glued to the TV."

The plan for the first night of the air campaign was a "multi-pronged attack across Iraq's air defense network." F-117 Stealth Fighters would hit key targets over Baghdad while the F-15E Strike Eagles would fly lower-altitude missions against the H-2 and H-3 airfields. Unlike the pure air superiority F-15Cs, the F-15E Strike Eagles were multi-purpose "strike fighters," capable of both air superiority and air-to-ground missions. Throughout Desert Storm, however, they were used almost exclusively in the latter role. Meanwhile, the EF-111 electronic warfare planes would fly in low, jamming the Iraqis' surveillance and air defense radars (all without fighter escort) to facilitate the F-117's ingress and egress. "Contrary to popular belief," said Rick Tollini, "stealth technology did not mean that the F-117s were invisible to radars, just low observable."

But once the F-117s, F-15Es, and the attendant cruise missiles had found their mark, the coalition would no longer have the element of surprise. Having been alerted to the incoming bombardment, the Iraqis would scramble their MiG-25s, MiG-29s, and Mirage F1s to interdict the Allied aircraft.

The 58th Fighter Squadron, however, would be waiting for them.

As the initial wave of F-117s and Strike Eagles egressed from Iraqi airspace, the 58th would sweep north, clearing the skies of any enemy aircraft that responded to the initial bombardment.

In the pre-dawn hours of January 17, Rick Tollini recalled that: "The mission brief went pretty smoothly. There actually was not much to go over because we had analyzed and pre-briefed this mission so many times in the last couple of weeks. We really just needed a quick review and to update the weather for that night. But it was actually the weather that generated some of the greatest concern."

Indeed, Murphy's Law was about to strike a tender nerve.

The squadron's weather officer delivered news that *no* fighter pilot wanted to hear: A cold front had descended over Saudi Arabia, creating a heavy nighttime cloud cover with "embedded thunderstorms up to 35,000 feet" covering the aerial routes to and from the Stratotankers. This bad weather wasn't enough to ground the mission but, as Rick Tollini noted, "There is absolutely nothing more terrifying to a fighter pilot than the thought of refueling off a tanker at night and in adverse weather."

To make matters worse, the KC-135 pilots had been instructed not to perform any refuels on "auto-pilot." Apparently, several KC-135s had been experiencing auto-pilot malfunctions, and they had been ordered to conduct all refuels while flying manually. "Trying to get into position for the air refueling," said Tollini, "while the KC–135 was flown hands-on (no auto-pilot), at night and in bad weather, was going to be like trying to mount a bucking bronco after it had already come out of the gate … with a blindfold on."

Another concern was the anticipated "rollover" of the squadron's Mode 4 Automated Airborne Interrogator (AAI) system. As Tollini recalled: "The AAI allowed a friendly aircraft with the correct code to respond to another aircraft's electronic 'query' regarding its position. If the response was within the other aircraft's radar scope field of regard, he could see the friendly reply on his radar scope, displayed as a diamond shape or circle. The system provided simple positional situation awareness and identification." Essentially, the AAI allowed the F-15s to determine which aircraft were friendly, and which aircraft were enemy. It was part of the broader "Identification Friend-or-Foe" (IFF) control measures that pilots would use in flight. "The Mode 4 was the most secure IFF interrogator mode we had. We relied on this system heavily to make sure we did not accidently fire on any friendly US aircraft."

The universal policy was that each unit would change its Mode 4 operating codes every 24 hours at midnight, Greenwich Mean Time (GMT). But in Saudi Arabia, 12:00 GMT was 3:00 AM, the exact time the 58th Fighter Squadron would be pushing across the Iraqi border. There was concern that the F-15E Strike Eagles would forget to rollover their Mode 4 operating codes at the appropriate GMT time. Without the latest codes, the friendly Strike Eagles wouldn't be able to identify themselves to the F-15Cs, thus increasing the likelihood of fratricide.

"One of the flight members was told to get a quick message off to Riyadh," said Tollini, "to tell the orbiting AWACS E-3 control aircraft to be sure to tell the earlier missions to change their Mode 4 code on time." None of the pilots in the 58th knew if the message would make it to the Strike

Eagle units on time, and the fear of fratricide would linger throughout the rest of the air war.

The eight F-15s taking off from Tabuk were divided into two, four-ship flights codenamed PENNZOIL and CITGO. "I am not sure why the combat planners chose major petroleum corporation names for our F-15 missions," said Tollini. "Normally those call-signs would have been the domain of the air refueling tankers, but these particular call-signs had a nice ring to them and were easy to say and hear in the heat of combat communications."

Tollini was the mission commander for this initial sortie and the flight lead for the PENNZOIL flight. Alongside him was his friend and wingman Larry "Cherry" Pitts; Mark "Willie" Williams; and Jon "JB" Kelk. The CITGO formation would be led by Rob "Cheese" Graeter. His wingman was Scott "Papa" Maw; and Bill "Tonic" Thiel would occupy the third position of the four-ship flight with Robert "LA" Brooks covering his wing. In the Air Force, it was not uncommon for a squadron commander to fly subordinate roles within a tactical formation. During these sorties, it was the flight leads and mission commanders who called the shots, irrespective of rank.

Members of the PENNZOIL flight were driven to the "Death Valley" parking area, while the CITGO flight crews were driven to "Disneyland." Todd McGirr and his maintenance teams had given "Death Valley" its name because the parking area had nothing more than a "barren shack (no toilets or running water), spiders, snakes, and four F-15C Eagles." On the other side of the runway, at "Disneyland," Graeter and his CITGO flight readied their F-15s for combat. Graeter would be the first to take off from the runway that morning.

"As I was getting strapped into my jet with the help of my crew chief," recalled Tollini, "Cheese's four Eagles started blasting off the runway right next to us in full afterburner, combat loaded, with a mighty roar. It was a stark reminder of what we were about to do. My crew chief looked me in the eye (almost like he thought he might not see me, or his jet, again) and said 'Good luck, Sir. Come back safe.' I just gave him a nod and said, 'Thanks. I will.'"

As the PENNZOIL and CITGO flights departed from Tabuk, Rick Tollini decided to tighten their formation in order to facilitate closer visual spacing. "Normally, in bad weather I would rather leave the flight members strung out in a long trail formation, allowing each jet to maintain 1–2 nautical miles separation using their radars." But tonight was different, as they were operating under Emission Control (EMCON) procedures, which meant limited use of radars and radio comms.

The first stop on their mission into Iraq was a rendezvous with the KC-135s, "which were far enough south that we would be out of sight of Iraq's long-range air defense surveillance radars." After refueling, PENNZOIL and CITGO would vector north to the same area where they had done their DCA patrols throughout Desert Shield. Essentially, they wanted the Iraqis to think it was just another routine cycle of Allied air patrols.

It didn't take long for PENNZOIL or CITGO to find the lingering Stratotanker. When Tollini arrived with the PENNZOIL flight, Graeter's team was "already on the wings of the KC-135 getting their pre-mission fuel top-off." As Graeter and his wingmen cleared the tanker, he radioed Tollini that they were going to head to their assigned orbiting area and look for better weather. "I told Cheese I would contact him on the radio when my flight was done refueling," said Rick. But, as expected, the lack of auto-pilot made for a *very* turbulent refuel process. "I am not sure if it

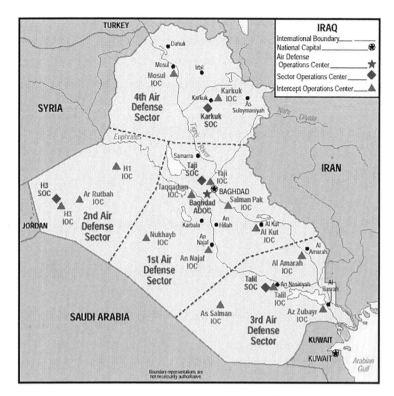

A map of the Iraqi airfields and air defense sectors, 1990.

was the pilot or co-pilot flying, but his or her attempts to keep the airplane level and on altitude resulted in more of an erratic, up-and-down porpoise-like pitching," he recalled. "After multiple attempts, I finally had to break radio silence and tell the tanker pilot, 'If you don't fly a little smoother, we are not going to be able to get our gas, and we won't be able to complete our mission.'"

At that point, the tanker pilot must have engaged his "auto-pilot" function because the KC-135 immediately leveled out, which made for a quick and easy refuel. As Mark Williams (the last wingman of the PENNZOIL flight) completed his top-off, Tollini switched his radio over to the AWACS frequency. "And it seemed that all Hell broke loose."

At 3:00 AM local time, PENNZOIL received an urgent radio call arrived from the nearby AWACS.

"PUSH NOW!"

Almost instinctively, Tollini replied: "Negative."

PENNZOIL was still fifteen minutes away from their anticipated start time. Moreover, they had to regroup with Rob Graeter's CITGO flight before pushing northward. When Tollini asked the AWACS controller why they were demanding an earlier push time, he said that they had detected enemy fighters scrambling from the southern airfields; "and this would put them right in the path of the Strike Eagles that had just hit the H-2/H-3 airfields." These F-15Es were now egressing from Iraqi airspace, heading southeast on a low-altitude flight plan.

Almost immediately, Rick Tollini's thoughts harkened back to his planning days during Desert Shield. He had met with that F-15E squadron a few months earlier to coordinate operations and ensure deconfliction of ingress/egress routes. Tollini had warned them that their egress routes took them too close to the Mudaysis Air Base, where the IQAF had several fighters on alert-scramble status. "I pointed this out to the F-15E mission commander and I suggested he should exit Iraq due south and across the Saudi border," thus avoiding any potential intercepts from the MiGs at Mudaysis. "He told me they didn't have the gas to do that, and although I had plotted it out as the same time and distance to cover, I did not want to second-guess him. I also had no authority over his mission planning."

But now, it was obvious that Tollini had been right all along.

These bandits were closing in fast on the egressing F-15Es. PENNZOIL had to intercept.

Still, the AWACS's call for an "early push" was problematic

for Tollini. The Strike Eagles were still in the area, which would make for some very crowded airspace. Naturally, this increased the probability of fratricide. "I checked in with Cheese and his CITGO flight and found out they were about 60 nautical miles south of the Push point. Cheese had taken his flight farther south to find some clear weather and had planned to turn north in a few more minutes to hit his Push point on time. Now, we didn't have the time."

Realizing that they couldn't wait to rendezvous with CITGO, Tollini ordered all eight F-15s to intercept the incoming bandits.

"PENNZOIL, CITGO. Fence In! ... we're pushing now!"

Acknowledging the call, every pilot switched his Master Arm into the "hot" position, actively arming each missile and gun aboard his plane. "PENNZOIL and CITGO flight headed north into a situation that would now be totally different from that originally planned." These eight F-15s were supposed to be in a linear formation, travelling abreast. But now, given the position of Graeter's CITGO flight, PENNZOIL was about 50 nautical miles in front, offset to the east.

But their relative spacing wasn't the biggest problem.

When Tollini glanced at his radar, he could see the telltale circular icons of a friendly Mode 4 Interrogation reply. The F-15Es had indeed rolled over to the new Mode 4 operating codes but, just as he had predicted, they were passing right by the Mudaysis Air Base. And the enemy bandits were on their way.

Pushing forward into a linear "Wall of Eagles" formation, JB Kelk and his PENNZOIL wingmen flew northward, scanning their radars and listening intently to the radio traffic. "The radios got very busy on the strike frequency," he recalled, "and it was hard to get a word in edgewise."

Suddenly, Kelk's radar showed the blip of an incoming aircraft.

A bandit? - he wondered.

At a distance of 40 miles north, and an altitude of 7,000 feet, its relative position indicated that it was likely an enemy bandit. "I tried to get the AWACS to confirm...but had no luck. I was still very concerned about frat [fratricide], but even without the AWACS's help, I was confident that this was a bad guy. He was heading south towards me and climbing." Indeed, by the time Kelk readied his first missile, the bandit was at 17,000 feet. "Once I was in parameters," he said, "I fired a single AIM-7." As soon as Kelk depressed the trigger, he closed his eyes, not wanting the white flash of the missile to rob him of his night vision. "We had flown a lot of nights during the pre-war time in Saudi and were very good at flying nights in the pre-NVG [night vision goggles] era, and I didn't want to risk it."

After deploying his missile, however, Kelk was unsure of whether the AIM-7 had met its target. "I look out the front and I see a purple-blueish light on the horizon"—not the telltale orange fireball he had been expecting. "After about three to five seconds, it fades." Kelk was bewildered.

Did he kill the bandit?

Was this purple-blue ember the skewed sight of an explosion?

Had the enemy bandit been dropping flares?

"At night, you can't judge the distance, he said, "so I just wasn't certain." He did a radar search of the immediate area and found nothing. Whoever this bandit may have been, he had now disappeared from radar view.

To make matters worse, the instruments aboard Kelk's F-15 were malfunctioning. As was customary, Kelk was expected to jettison his external fuel tanks upon end-of-mission. The tanks, however, refused to come off. And the additional weight would undoubtedly slow him down when the rest of PENNZOIL sallied back into Saudi airspace.

Adding to this confusion was his onboard weapons panel.

Despite having fired an AIM-7 missile, the panel showed that all missiles were still attached to Kelk's wings. "I guess were about 75 miles south of Baghdad at this time," said Kelk. Although he had indeed fired a missile, he was unsure whether he had truly killed the faceless bandit. "I didn't call the splash for several reasons," he said. "The radios were still real busy, and I was more concerned with the next merge [rendezvous] than making a radio call. Also, with the conflicting cockpit indications I had been getting, I didn't feel that I was in a place to make that call."

However, after PENNZOIL had re-grouped and was back over Saudi airspace, Kelk called out to his wingman, Captain Mark "Willie" Williams, to visually inspect his missile rack. Flying alongside Kelk's wing, Williams confirmed that the AIM-7 was missing.

The weapons panel had been wrong; Kelk had indeed fired the AIM-7.

Back at the Tabuk airbase, and still unsure of his aerial victory, Kelk reported it as a "probable" kill. A few hours later, however, the AWACS that had been aloft with PENNZOIL sent its report to Tonic Thiel. Not only had Kelk destroyed the bandit, but the kill had been confirmed as a MiG-29.

Jon "JB" Kelk made history that night. He had achieved the first aerial kill of Desert Storm and the first-ever combat kill of a MiG-29.

But while Jon Kelk had been tussling with the MiG-29 (and his own malfunctioning instruments), Rob Graeter and his comrades in the CITGO flight had been exceptionally busy. Listening to the radio, Graeter had heard the same call from the AWACS, ordering PENNZOIL to intercept the incoming MiGs. But like Tollini, Rob Graeter realized that the early call would disrupt their original plan to engage the enemy on a 100-mile frontage. That premature deployment "really screwed us up," he said. "We would have had a much better picture if we had waited, since the idea was to get the MiGs airborne off their alert pads, chasing the strikers."

Still, the CITGO pilots decided to make the best of their situation and acknowledged the AWACS's call. According to the AWACS, these incoming bandits were MiG-29s, far north of Iraq's Mudaysis Airbase. Graeter "rogered" the call, but because the MiGs were more than 100 miles north, he could not yet see them on his own radar.

As CITGO pressed north towards the border, however, Graeter detected the egressing Strike Eagles. In fact, the F-15Es had just cleared their target areas.

Therein, however, lay the problem with PENNZOIL'S and CITGO'S early push: the densely crowded airspace. The four-ship flights would have "good guys mixed in with bad guys," whereas the original mission plan was to shoot from beyond visual range (BVR) within a relatively clear airspace.

As Graeter flew towards the Strike Eagles' egress corridor, the AWACS alerted him of an incoming threat near the vicinity of Mudaysis.

No surprises there, Graeter thought.

After all, CENTAF Intelligence knew that the Iraqis had forward-deployed their MiGs and Mirage F1s to the area. Thus, Graeter and his CITGO comrades had expected some of these bandits to take flight.

Simultaneous with the AWACS alert, however, Graeter

noticed a blip on his own radar screen—"about 22 to 25 miles off my nose heading northwest." He was certain that this was the same bandit that the AWACS had detected. Suddenly, Graeter's radar detected a second bandit in the air. Moments later, Graeter's wingman, Captain Scott "Papa" Maw, called out a third bandit.

The Iraqis now had three planes in the air.

Returning his focus to the lead bandit, Graeter noticed the Iraqi was climbing to 5,000 feet. "He was generally heading towards the track of the F-15Es," said Graeter. "We'll never know exactly what he was doing, but my guess was that he had been scrambled on the E models. If they [Iraqis] had any kind of radar, they would have known there was aircraft in the vicinity, but what kind of information or data he had…we'll obviously never know."

Watching the bandit from his radar screen, he saw the Iraqi fighter stabilize its descent at about 7,000 feet. Ramping down to intercept, Graeter jettisoned his fuel tanks to pick up speed and identified the bandit at 10 miles out.

It was an Iraqi Mirage F1.

Of the numerous planes in Iraq's inventory, the Mirage F1 was among the only respectable fighters. A French export, the F1 variants had found their way into the service of several Gulf State air forces. The Kuwaitis, Qataris, Jordanians, and even the Libyans had made extensive use of the Mirage fighter. During the Iran-Iraq War, Iranian F-14 pilots remembered that the Mirage F1 was the only Iraqi fighter that could truly hold its own in a dogfight.

Today, however, this Mirage F1 would fall victim to Cheese Graeter's missile.

Locking onto the Mirage, Graeter fired off his AIM-7. "Even though in academics we had always discussed not looking at the missile when you shoot to preserve your night vision, I looked." Thankfully, the flash didn't impact Graeter's night vision enough to prevent him from witnessing the "bright, yellow conical blast as the missile detonated." The blast, he recalled, "looked just like a cone because of the airspeed of the missile taking the flame forward. The eerie part of all of this is that there is no noise...so you get all this in visual only. It lit up the ground below and the cloud deck above, so it had an eerie look to it."

Moments later, Graeter witnessed a secondary explosion on the ground in the vicinity of the Mirage wreckage. Just as before, this explosion illuminated the ground below and the cloud cover above. Looking at the explosion, Graeter could see that it was the wreckage of *another* Mirage F1.

But Graeter was confused.

Neither he nor his wingman had shot down the second Mirage. How then, had the enemy bandit crashed?

Back at Tabuk, the unit's Chief of Intelligence confirmed that both offending aircraft had been Mirage F1s, and that the Iraqi Air Command had scrambled both in response to the F-15E strike packages. Later, it was determined that the second Mirage had crashed while reacting defensively to Graeter's killing of the first Mirage. Essentially, the second Mirage pilot was spooked by the sudden demise of his wingman, and subsequently crashed his own plane in a fit of panic. Thus, Rob Graeter was credited with *two* Mirage kills for January 17, 1991.

For the rest of their mission, the PENNZOIL and CITGO flights locked up a few more bandits, but many of these Iraqi fighters turned away as soon as they realized they were on the F-15's radar. "We continued on our planned route and soon were heading south for Saudi airspace and to avoid conflicting with follow-on waves of hundreds more fighters and bombers," said Rick Tollini. "When I knew that PENNZOIL and CITGO flights were safely across the border in friendly territory, I called for everybody to turn on all their exterior lights to a bright/flash mode. I was amazed as I looked out across the night sky to see my flight still in perfect formation, and right alongside to the west was Cheese and his CITGO flight. We came out in the perfect line-abreast 8-ship formation."

On the ground at Tabuk, the incoming flights landed to a chorus of cheers and excitement. "We already knew we had a kill...and a double-kill!" said Chief Matos. "That news spread like wildfire. And we immediately asked if we could paint stars on the airplanes"—designating confirmed kills. It was a coveted sign of respect among fighter pilots. "And we were allowed to do it," Matos added. For the crew chiefs and maintenance teams, these aerial victories were an immense point of pride. They had spent countless hours prepping these F-15s, and they wanted their planes to win. "I want my planes to fly and I want my planes to shoot down MiGs," Matos beamed.

As the PENNZOIL and CITGO planes entered their post-flight maintenance, the crew chiefs let Cheese Graeter and JB Kelk keep the missiles' umbilical cords as a memento. The cord from their first missile kill was a treasured keepsake among fighter pilots.

Emerging from their debrief shortly before dawn, Tollini, Graeter, and the other pilots headed back to their rooms for some much-needed sleep. Each of them would be going airborne again soon. The first daylight missions of Desert Storm were about to begin.

When Kelk and Graeter returned from their nighttime missions, Chuck Magill recalled: "I'll never forget the looks on their faces. They had all been shot at a bunch. They were tired, emotional, and pretty excited. I was envious, since they were now 'seasoned' combat pilots, and had their first real combat missions under their belts, and even a couple of kills."

Magill was now the mission commander for the first daylight sortie of the war. Today, the 58th would be covering a large-force strike mission. An entire wing of F-16s would be flying into Iraq (40 aircraft), accompanied by F-4 Wild Weasels and EF-111 Ravens: the former to suppress enemy air defenses; the latter to disrupt the Iraqis' radar network. The 58th Fighter Squadron (and elements from the 1st Fighter Wing) would have "overall charge of the air-to-air, pre-strike sweep and escort duties." According to the plan, an eight-ship formation from the 58th would sweep nearly 25-30 nautical miles ahead of the main body "strike package" and destroy any loitering Iraqi fighters.

"I started our briefing around 10:00 AM," said Magill, "and besides our eight guys [the second iteration of the CITGO and PENNZOIL flight groups], the wing commander [Rick Parsons] and a bunch of other folks were there. When Intel started briefing the enemy air defense picture—the heavily-defended target area to include the missile engagement zones—I looked over at my wingman, and his eyes were the size of silver dollars. I think I went through two bottles of water during that brief, my mouth was so dry." Magill was an accomplished aviator, but he had *never* been this nervous before, and he could tell that his wingman felt likewise. Nevertheless, Magill told him that as long as they watched each other's backs, they'd be fine.

The squadron's portion of the mission once again featured the CITGO and PENNZOIL callsigns, but this time with a few different pilots. Magill's CITGO four-ship would occupy the western sector, sweeping to the northwest side of Baghdad near the Al Asad Air Base, "one of Iraq's major fighter airfields and a likely source of enemy fighter activity." After CITGO had completed its sweep, Magill would take them to the southwest, looking for any Iraqi fighters trying to end-run the "strike package" aircraft from the rear.

PENNZOIL, meanwhile, would fly along the eastern flanks, sweeping towards Al Taqaddum, then to the southwestern border of Baghdad's SAM engagement zone. From there, PENNZOIL would vector back to the west, clearing the engagement area for the incoming strike package. "This flow plan was important to avoid the possibility of fratricide and not impact the strike package ingress route."

Climbing aboard his F-15, Magill recalled that the moment he ignited his engine, "all the nerves left. I just focused on the mission." Launching with the second iteration of the CITGO flight, Magill went airborne alongside PENNZOIL to his right flank. Almost immediately, the nearby AWACS alerted them of two incoming bogeys from the south.

Both were identified as MiG-29s.

"Those poor Fulcrum[6] pilots had to be the unluckiest guys ever to strap on a fighter jet," said Rick Tollini, who was commanding this iteration of the PENNZOIL flight. "I doubt they had any idea of what they were up against or what was coming their way, but if they had even an inkling of the approaching tsunami wave of Air Force fighters, then I would say they were probably the bravest pilots in the air that day."

As CITGO and PENNZOIL, continued pushing northward, it appeared that the MiGs were travelling north-south at a low altitude. "We could see the bandits on our radars," said Magill, "and we sampled them occasionally." As Magill's CITGO formation was targeting this group of MiGs, Tollini asked to break away from the combined flight

---

[6] "Fulcrum" was the MiG-29's NATO reporting name. Most Eastern Bloc aircraft were identified in the West by the reporting nicknames that NATO had given them. Soviet fighters were given nicknames beginning with "F," hence "Fulcrum."

group to reconnoiter the Al Asad Air Base a few miles northward. "It was important to monitor Al Asad," Magill said, "as it had over 70 fighters there, and it had not been hit the first night." Indeed, the Al Taqqadum and Al Assad air bases had a combined strength of more than 100 Iraqi fighters. MiGs from both bases had flown sorties during the first night of the air campaign, and Chuck Magill fully expected them to "launch the fleet" at the incoming F-15s. "They could have made it very interesting for us," he recalled, "even with eight Eagles."

After some brief consideration, Magill agreed to let Tollini inspect Al Asad. Moments later, however, Magill's radar erupted with the sound of incoming SAMs—"SA-2 and SA-3 SAMs targeting me." Magill started scanning the horizon for the telltale smoke trails, but saw that the sky was clear. Then, suddenly, one of Magill's wingmen, Tony "Kimo" Schiavi called out "Smoke in the air!"—indicating that the SAMs were now visible.

Jumping into survival mode, Magill ordered CITGO to jettison their external fuel tanks. Releasing their tanks as they arced into their dive, one of Magill's wingmen recalled the mesmerizing sight of "the eight tanks coming off in perfect unison while we broke away and down." Magill and his comrades dove for more than 15,000 feet, picking up speed as they evaded the incoming SAMs. As it turned out, CITGO had stumbled across an Iraqi ground unit—"and all they had to do to see us was look up, so they targeted us. I'm not sure how many missiles were shot, since I never saw them."

Magill later recalled that, up to this point, everything about the mission had seemed sterile—"just like another training mission"—until his Master Alarm went off. "That really got my attention," he said. "This wasn't a training mission, and they're trying to kill us! That's when the intensity really ramped up. I've got a lot of speed now, and the Eagle cockpit is loud like a freight train, the radios are going off...and we're only 30 miles from a merge with one of the best enemy fighters in the world."

After evading the SAMs, Magill radioed the AWACS, asking them to confirm the bearing and range to the MiG-29. Turning his formation onto a 30-degree heading, Magill soon detected the bandits at 30 miles out. "As we get into 22 miles," he recalled, "the bandits turned cold," meaning that the Iraqis were now turning away from the F-15s and heading northward.

"I'm thinking: This is it," said Magill.

"They [the MiGs] are going to land, launch the fleet at us, open up all the SAM sites and shred us—but they don't."

Thus, Magill decided to run the bandits down.

"We all go to full afterburner and accelerate out." Closing within 16 miles, the bandits suddenly turned back to meet the F-15s head on—accelerating to 600 knots. At fourteen miles, Rhory Draeger, got radar lock on one of the MiGs—firing a single AIM-7.

"Fox 1!" Draeger cried.

The Sparrow missile found its mark on one of the bandits, striking the MiG right through its canopy. Magill, meanwhile, set his own radar lock onto the second MiG—"showing about 1,250 knots closure."

From a distance of 12 miles, Magill fired his own AIM-7.

"I'd shot a lot of 2.75 folding fin rockets in the [F-18] Hornet, and sometimes the fins don't work, and they go off like bottle rockets, going crazy. I had also shot a lot of AIM-7s, but this one came off and went straight for the ground." Not impressed by the AIM-7's wild trajectory, Magill lined up another shot and fired his second Sparrow of the day. "I had read a lot of Vietnam reports, and many guys had reported time compression during the stress of combat." In other words, time itself appeared to slow down during the heat of battle. "Well," said Magill, "this is where I experienced it firsthand. As the second missile came off, everything went silent. The missile appeared to be in slow motion. I could see the yellow and brown band, the slow roll as it went out slowly. Then, at about 10 seconds time to go on the second shot, it was like someone turned all the volumes back up."

But, as it turned out, Magill's first missile (the missile with the seemingly errant trajectory), corrected itself and impacted the MiG just below its right wing. As the MiG started lurching downward, Magill's second missile (the one he had purportedly seen in slow motion) went right through the middle of the MiG-29's fuselage. "The explosion wasn't as big as I would have expected," he recalled, "just more of a sparkle and a flash."

Clearing the area, Magill called to the nearby AWACS: "Splash 2! Splash 2!"—indicating that both MiGs had been destroyed. The euphoria was short-lived, however, as Magill's radar soon lit up with more SAM warnings. "We were right in the middle of the Baghdad MEZ [missile engagement zone]." Looking out from his canopy, Magill could see the boosters and smoke trails from the incoming SA-2, SA-3, and SA-6 missiles. Breaking off in an evasive maneuver, Magill jettisoned his centerline fuel tank and expended the rest of his chaff, hoping to confuse the missiles as they ascended into the sky. "I saw three of them," Magill said, "but there were probably more; it was hard to count them, since they were all stacked on top of each other." But however many SAMs there may have been, Magill and his comrades successfully evaded them and returned safely to Tabuk.

Magill's aerial victory that day made him the first Marine aviator since Vietnam to down an enemy plane in combat. After the war, Chuck Magill gave several presentations on

his air-to-air victory at the Navy Fighter Weapons School—
the world-renowned "Top Gun." During one of the Top
Gun briefings, Magill discovered why the Iraqi MiGs had
suddenly turned back towards the F-15s after previously
withdrawing to the north. These MiGs had actually been
trying to chase down a flight of Navy F-14s that were
coming out of western Iraq. The prowling MiGs, however,
had run right into Magill and his comrades in the Citgo
flight. "Turns out that the F-14s had the MiGs about nine
miles behind them, and were about to turn back into them
when they saw us go over the top, shooting missiles. We
never saw the Tomcats!"

Meanwhile, Rick Tollini recalled that: "The highlight of
that mission for me actually came shortly after I landed back
at Tabuk. After taxiing my jet out into the Death Valley
parking area near the approach end of the runway, I climbed
down the ladder and started to organize my gear to catch a
ride back to our operations building." Colonel Parsons, the
wing commander, had already arrived at Death Valley,
presumably for a quick debrief and to congratulate the
incoming flights on a job well done. As Colonel Parsons
walked up to Tollini, however, Magill's CITGO flight
began its final approach to the runway. "This was the first
daytime mission where we had shot down some enemy
aircraft," said Tollini; and he wondered if Magill or Draeger
would commit to performing a "Victory Roll." As Tollini
described, the Victory Roll was a low-flying aileron roll
over the runway. It was the "traditional fighter-pilot method
of demonstrating to the airfield they had just downed an
adversary." Although not a safe maneuver by any means,
wartime commanders occasionally permitted Victory Rolls
so long as the surrounding airspace was clear. But, as Tollini
admitted, this was "not our fathers' Air Force." A Victory
Roll in the modern-day Air Force might be enough to get a
pilot grounded or, even worse, stripped of his wings.

But Chuck Magill, still high on achieving his first aerial kill, was determined to execute the daring deed. As Tollini and Parsons began to chat, Tollini caught a sidelong glance of Magill's plane as he "came around his final turn with his landing gear down in what looked like an ordinary landing approach. But, just as he came in over the threshold of the runway, and right before his wheels touched down I watched, amazed, as Sly slapped his gear back up, plugged the jet into afterburner, pulled up the nose...and performed a beautiful slow roll, right there in front of the whole world, and Col Parsons."

Tollini was amused; Parsons was not.

Looking over at the wing commander, "I saw his jaw locked tight, turning five shades of red, and a laser beam stare penetrating Sly's Eagle. It didn't get any better when Hoser performed the exact same maneuver following Sly." Tollini was certain that Parsons was going to explode at both pilots as soon as they landed. "But just then," Tollini said, "the entire crowd of crew chiefs and weapons troops out in Death Valley (and all across the airfield) let out the biggest whooping and hollering we'd heard since the day we arrived in Tabuk." In the Air Force, it was widely understood that the planes "belonged" to the maintenance crews; the pilots simply "borrowed" them. There was no denying that Matos, McGirr, and their maintenance troops were thrilled at the sight of another Eagle returning with its missile racks empty. And the Victory Roll had only amplified their enthusiasm. Looking back at Colonel Parsons, Tollini saw the wing commander shake his head and walk away. "That was his way of giving tacit (even if uninvited) approval for his boys to do Victory Rolls after any daytime kills."

Chief Matos, took in all eight planes for their post-flight maintenance. "And we had those planes turned around within 30 minutes"—meaning that each F-15 was checked, serviced, rearmed, refueled, and labeled "ready" for the next mission. "For the first day of the air war," he said," we flew more missions than we had planes." Such was the level of synergy and efficiency between the pilots and their crews.

"I was not involved in the first 24 hours' worth of big packages," said ET Murphy. "Those were the missions where every flight got a kill or two. After that first day, opposition was very sporadic. I drove around Iraq trying to find trouble but there was no action. It was really frustrating." Little did Murphy know, however, that within the next two weeks, he would become one of the few pilots in Desert Storm to achieve a double-kill. "Our missions varied from DCA," he continued, "where we flew race-track pattern to protect the AWACS and tankers behind us, to a sweep where he drove around Iraq looking for trouble. We even flew in the [contrails] to advertise: 'Here we are, come get us.' But we didn't get any takers." Other times, Murphy and his wingmen flew into Iraqi airspace "just to cause trouble," as he said, hoping to lure out any surviving MiGs.

Sadly, after the first night of the air war, the 58th Fighter Squadron learned that one of their Navy comrades had been shot down. An F/A-18 Hornet piloted by Lieutenant Commander Scott Speicher had been downed by an enemy plane. It was the first time an American F/A-18 had been lost to enemy fire. At first, it was widely reported that Speicher had been hit by a surface-to-air missile, but the Department of Defense later confirmed that he had been shot down by an Iraqi MiG-25 Foxbat.

Shortly after 3:00 AM on January 17, US naval air squadrons from the *Kennedy* and *Saratoga* sent a combined "strike package" into Iraq. Their collective mission was to suppress enemy air defenses and destroy key facilities at the Tammuz Air Base. Leading this strike package into Iraq were ten F/A-18 Hornets from Squadrons VFA-81 and VFA-83, flying from the *Saratoga*. As the lead element in the strike force, these ten Hornets crossed the Saudi border arrayed in a "wall" formation. Each Hornet maintained a horizontal distance of 2-5 miles from another, while keeping a vertical distance of 1,000 feet between each plane.

The F/A-18s swept ahead of the main strike force (consisting of twelve Grumman A-6 Intruders), providing front cover and suppression of the enemy's forward air defense. Once within range of Tammuz, however, the ten Hornets arrayed themselves into a fan formation, preparing to launch their anti-radiation missiles at the designated targets. Following behind were eight of the twelve A-6 Intruders, each of which initiated its bombing run from 25,000 feet, delivering their Mk84 2,000-lb bombs. The remaining four A-6s followed with a volley of GBU-10 Laser-Guided Bombs, destroying two prominent MiG-29 shelters.

Although the strike package had liquidated its first target, the Iraqi radar stations had detected their approach. When the A-6s and F/A-18s initially entered Iraqi airspace, the only Iraqi fighters in the sky were MiG-29s, all of whom were preoccupied with chasing a flight of American B-52s. When the Tammuz radar station determined that the F/A-18s were headed north to Qadessiya Air Base, the No. 84 Squadron scrambled a MiG-25 to intercept.

Scott Speicher, meanwhile, was flying at the tail end of the Hornets' echelon formation. As he approached the designated launch point, he disengaged auto-pilot and descended to 27,872 feet, preparing to launch his anti-radiation missiles. Little did he realize, however, that the incoming MiG-25 was about to get a lock on him.

The Iraqi pilot fired his R-40 missile, which detonated just short of Speicher's aircraft, below the left side of the cockpit. The blast from the 154-lb warhead, however, flung the F/A-18 nearly 60 degrees to its right, causing a 6G turn that sheared off the plane's fuel tanks and one of Speicher's unfired missiles. The ailing Hornet plummeted into the desert floor, crashing about 40 miles south of the Qadessiya Air Base. Although a few of Speicher's wingmen had seen his descent, none were certain if he had been killed or had ejected. The following day, Speicher was officially listed as "Missing in Action." Three months after the end of Desert Storm, however, Speicher's status was updated to "Killed in Action/Body Not Recovered." For the next several years, his fate remained a mystery. Eventually, the Iraqi government permitted recovery of the F/A-18 wreckage, but claimed to know nothing of Speicher's status or his whereabouts.

In December 1993, Qatari officials discovered the wreckage of Speicher's aircraft. From this, it was determined that Speicher had ejected from the plane and may have been alive for several hours after his ejection. In April 1994, satellite photography revealed human-made symbols on the desert floor near the Hornet's crash site—quite possibly Speicher's "Escape and Evade" sign. A year later, the International Red Cross, sponsored an excavation of the crash site, but found no conclusive evidence regarding Speicher's fate.

For several years, the US Navy officially maintained that Speicher had been downed by an Iraqi SAM. Many of Speicher's comrades, however, openly doubted the "official story." One pilot, who flew alongside Speicher during the same mission, publicly stated: "I'm telling you right now, don't believe what you're being told. It was that MiG that shot [Speicher] down." Rumors abounded that Speicher was still alive and being held prisoner in Iraq. Following the US-led invasion of Iraq in 2003, however, American authorities determined that Speicher had never been captured by the Iraqi government. A break in the case finally came in 2009.

Acting on a tip from an Iraqi local in the Anbar Province, a team of US Navy and Marine personnel unearthed the remains of Scott Speicher. According to the informant, Speicher had been buried by local Bedouins who had discovered his body. After confirming that the remains were indeed Speicher's, he was given a proper burial with full military honors at Arlington National Cemetery.

Although saddened by the loss of a fellow aviator, Larry Pitts and Rick Tollini partially avenged Speicher's death by shooting down two other MiG-25s on January 19, 1991.

"The 19th was day three of the war," said Larry Pitts, "and the missions just kept coming." Rick Tollini added that: "Hundreds of targets had been hit and nine Iraqi fighters had already been shot down," five of which had been downed by the 58th Fighter Squadron. "Some of us were on our fourth or fifth combat missions, with precious little sleep in between."

On the Iraqi side of the border, Saddam Hussein was already against the ropes. Several of his air defense sites had been destroyed, along with several more Command & Control nodes. At airbases across Iraq, much of the Iraqi Air Force was being destroyed before it even got off the ground. Meanwhile, the "Butcher of Baghdad" began firing Scud missiles into Israel, hoping to bring the Israelis into the conflict, and fracture the coalition along religious lines. Although the Scuds were a persistent nuisance, they were notoriously inaccurate. Many of them were intercepted by US Patriot missiles or landed harmlessly in the Mediterranean. General H. Norman Schwarzkopf, the commander of UN forces in the Gulf, once quipped that he was more afraid of being struck by lightning than being hit by a Scud missile.

For the men of the 58th, their mission on the morning of January 19 had been to cover a strike force of F-16s delivering conventional munitions to airfields and other targets in western Iraq. Sadly, that mission was cancelled due to poor weather over the target areas. "There was a low undercast of solid clouds stretching from the Saudi border as far north as we could see toward Baghdad."

In the wake of that canceled mission, however, Rick Tollini received an urgent call from CENTAF Headquarters in Riyadh. On the other end was Captain Richard "Spad" McSpadden, one of Tollini's old friends from the 12th Fighter Squadron in Okinawa. Spad was now working in the Combat Operations cell at CENTAF and was responsible for coordinating the F-15C missions in theater. "Kluso," he said, "I need four Eagles to fly a CAP in the vicinity of H-2/H-3 airfields [western Iraq]. The Iraqis shot a bunch of Scud missiles at Israel last night and the Israelis are pissed. We're going to send up a bunch of strike aircraft to do some Scud hunting. We need somebody out there in a couple of hours to fly a CAP to protect the strikers. Can you guys do it?"

Given that their prior mission with the F-16s had been cancelled, Tollini saw an opportunity for his four-ship flight to get some more air time. Before saying "Yes," however, Tollini told Spad that he would check with his wingmen and with Chief Matos to see if the squadron could support the pop-up mission. Not surprisingly, all of Kluso's wingmen (Pitts, Kelk, and Williams) were up for the mission; and Matos gave his customary "can do" reply for making the planes mission-ready.

Tollini called back McSpadden, telling him that the four-ship flight was a "Go."

"Then we hit the Tabuk flight-line kitchen for a pancake breakfast," Tollini said, "did a quick flight brief during the meal, and by the time we were done eating our jets were ready for us." These pancakes were a welcomed break from the typical fare served at the Tabuk mess hall. "There really wasn't much good to eat around Tabuk," said Tollini, and the Western-style fare was limited. But shortly after the squadron's arrival in Saudi Arabia, a group of Pakistani contractors set up a mobile kitchen along the flight line, open 24-hours a day, serving all ranks and workers. "While they also did not have much to cook," said Tollini, "and made possibly the worst hamburgers known to mankind, there was one menu item at which they excelled...pancake." Tollini said "pancake" in the singular because one pancake was all he needed for a fulfilling meal. "They were HUGE," he said, "the size of a large dinner plate and about three-quarter inch thick. It did not take long for the popularity of the Tabuk flight-line kitchen to grow, and soon there were long lines of customers, even in the dead of night."

Going airborne for the "Scud hunt," Tollini's four-ship formation included Larry Pitts, JB Kelk, and Mark Williams. "We carried the CITGO call-sign with us on this day," he said, and "rendezvoused with our air refueling tanker to top off our tanks before proceeding to our planned orbit area. We really did not know what to expect but, I assumed this would be a routine and uneventful mission for us."

Little did he know that this mission would be anything but routine.

Indeed, the CITGO flight had barely arrived on station when they received a call from the AWACS. "He advised us that there was a very large US Navy strike package that was going to be passing directly through our CAP area enroute to a target near Baghdad." Not wanting to obstruct the Navy's ingress, or appear like a potential target to an incoming F-14, Tollini moved his flight farther west and watched the Navy strike force pass them by.

But about thirty minutes later, AWACS appeared on the radio again, alerting CITGO to a group of bandits flying in pursuit of the egressing F-14s. Answering the call, Pitts,

Tollini, Kelk, and Williams dropped their wing-mounted fuel tanks and pressed northeast. "Things were about to happen very quickly, with nothing to fall back on except teamwork and experience." CITGO's direction of travel would allow the Navy jets to bypass them, "and as we approached their 6 o'clock from the west we could turn north to engage the Iraqi fighters."

The next few moments played out exactly how Pitts and Tollini had anticipated. The Navy strike package cleared the area, and as CITGO turned north, both men picked up radar contacts at 50 nautical miles. At first, the AWACS identified the bandits as MiG-29s. The MiG-29's AA-10A missile was comparable in performance to the AIM-7; so it might be a fair fight in terms of firepower, but the AWACS had identified only two bandits; so CITGO had the numerical advantage.

Ramping down to about 10,000 feet and closing the distance within 30 nautical miles, Larry Pitts started running sample radar locks onto the bandits, seeing how they might react. Just as he had anticipated, every time Pitts engaged his radar lock, "they would break the lock [i.e., moving out of radar range], so it was obvious they were aware of us, and probably had good radar warning gear." But soon thereafter, CITGO received another call from the AWACS: "Two more bandits airborne at low altitude ID MiG-29s." There were now *four* bandits in the air: the two bandits who had just broken away from Pitts' radar lock, and the two additional fighters that had just populated on the AWACS radar.

Tollini had seen these tactics before; and he knew there was a historical precedent behind them. Having studied Soviet Air Force tactics and after-action reports from the Iran-Iraq War, "I recognized what I was seeing as a possible decoy maneuver by the Iraqi formation." By turning away from the CITGO flight, these bandits were trying to lure the F-15s into a pursuit. "If we flowed to the northeast to follow the first fighters," Tollini continued, "it would allow the new enemy aircraft, the ones that AWACs called out to the north, to outflank our left side and come around the corner to ambush us from behind." This was a common tactic for the Iraqi Air Force, and they had used it with success against Iranian F-14 Tomcats and F-4 Phantoms.

But, as Tollini noted: "The difference today was that we were not Iranian fighter pilots and we weren't flying Tomcats and Phantoms. Both the F-14 and F-4 had problems with their radars in a 'look-down' mode, trying to find targets down low below their own altitude. The other factor in our favor was our intelligence on the Iraqi tactics, as well as many hours of experience gained against our own Aggressors [at Red Flag] and other simulated adversaries, who would test us against these types of tactics."

Thus, instead of following the decoys, Tollini vectored the CITGO flight back north to stiff-arm the decoying MiGs, choosing instead to focus on the trailing bandits. "Before we could make our final radar locks, however, the second group of bandits also started to maneuver: first a turn to the west and then a turn due north away from us." Tollini thought that perhaps this second group of MiGs wasn't interested in a fight, until they "quickly turned another 180 degrees right back to south, flying head-on to our flight."

As Pitts and Tollini closed in on the group, the bandits descended even lower—to 3,000 feet—"and heading due south of us in a three to five-mile lead-trail formation." Soon, the MiGs descended even lower—to 500 feet (unusual considering that the latter-day MiGs performed better at higher altitudes). Diving deeply to meet the elusive bandit, Larry Pitts broke through the clouds and visually identified the planes not as MiG-29s...but as MiG-25s.

Setting his radar lock on the MiG, Pitts knew that from this distance and altitude, it would be harder for the Foxbat to shake him. Still, the Iraqi pilot tried breaking to the right. "Not that the turning radius of a Foxbat doing 700 knots is very impressive," said Pitts, "but he tried."

Staying inside the MiG-25's turning circle, Pitts got a good tone for his AIM-9 Sidewinder. Pitts fired the AIM-9, but the MiG deployed its flares, which disrupted the missile's tracking system. Unfazed, Pitts thumbed the selector switch to his AIM-7 Sparrow and, despite getting good tone, the missile sailed right over the Foxbat's canopy. "He continues his turn and rolls out heading north, now doing about 500 knots."

Switching back to his AIM-9, Pitts was determined to kill the bandit. Once again, he heard the audible tone of "missile lock," but the Foxbat's warning system must have alerted the Iraqi pilot, because he deployed another set of flares before Pitts could even fire, thus negating the missile's tracker before it even left the wing. Frustrated by the preemptive decoy, Pitts hastily reset the AIM-9 and fired it, only to see the hurtling missile deflected by a *third* set of flares.

By now, Pitts could tell that the Foxbat pilot was getting desperate—and Pitts himself was getting agitated. Switching back to the AIM-7, Pitts fired the missile and watched in amazement as it tracked right into the Foxbat's engine, demolishing the tail of the aircraft. "His ejection seat comes out," Pitts recalled, "and I almost hit it, going right over the top of my canopy. I never saw him separate from the seat, or a chute, but I wouldn't want to test an ejection seat at 300 feet!" Indeed, at an altitude of 300 feet, and travelling at more than 500 knots, it was doubtful that the parachute would have deployed in time.

Tollini, meanwhile, set his sights squarely on the second MiG. Thrusting his F-15 to full afterburner, Tollini chased down the MiG-25, lining up an AIM-7 for his first missile shot. But his anticipation turned to disgust when the missile fell harmlessly onto the desert floor—"we think the rocket motor failed to light." Thumbing forward to the AIM-9, Tollini then launched his Sidewinder missile. Because he was so close to the elusive Foxbat, Tollini recalled that the heat-seeker tone was "just screaming at the huge infrared heat signature from the Foxbat's burners." As the AIM-9 traced towards its target, "I observed what looked to be a single flare come out of the back end of the Foxbat in front of me." This was not the normal cluster of flares (such as Larry Pitts had seen from his own Foxbat), but rather a single flare. Still, it was enough to get Tollini's attention, and enough to cause concern that the AIM-9 would vector off its target. He was pleased to see the missile track directly onto the MiG, but "it seemed to miss just slightly behind the burner plumes of the Foxbat and the warhead never detonated."

Thumbing back to his AIM-7, Tollini fired another shot, hearing "the train-like rumble of the Sparrow's rocket motor," he said, "and soon the missile appeared out in front of me and started a smooth and rapid acceleration toward the target. In his own words, he described the AIM-7's flight path as a "beautiful arcing turn from the outside of the Foxbat's own turn circle, almost like it had its own conscious mind and was trying to mimic the flight path of the MiG-25 in front. The AIM-7 was so much faster at this range (less than a mile now) that it rapidly caught up with its target."

As he watched the AIM-7 glide away from his wing, Tollini experienced the same phenomenon mentioned by Chuck Magill: time dilation. The sequence of events devolved into extreme slow-motion accompanied by tunnel vision/hearing. "Things that would normally be over in an instant stretched out now to what seemed like tens of seconds or even minutes," he said. "The tunnel vision/hearing just seemed to block out almost everything but my own breathing and the radio communication between me and my flight." Seeing the missile sail towards the MiG, Tollini felt as though it took several minutes. However, it was mere seconds before the Sparrow met its mark on the MiG-25, puncturing the plane's underbelly and sending the Foxbat to the desert floor in a spectacular fireball.

"From there we made our way back to Tabuk," recalled Tollini, "reporting into our operations about our missile expenditures"—he and Pitts had fired eight total missiles against the two Foxbats—"so they knew we were probably coming back with some confirmed kills." As they made their final descent into Tabuk, nearly everyone in the squadron had gathered near the runway to see if the incoming four-ship would do some Victory Rolls.

"Cherry and I did not disappoint them."

When Pitts and Tollini taxied into their parking spots at the Disneyland shelters, they could see that the maintenance troops were excited. As Tollini's crew chief helped him out of the jet, he asked: "How many?"

Tollini held up two fingers—one for his own kill; the other for Larry Pitts' kill.

"The weapons crews were pulling the spent missile umbilicals off the weapons stations and keeping them as souvenirs," although they let Tollini keep the souvenir from his AIM-9. Years later, he passed it along to his father.

That same day—January 19, 1991—Cesar "Rico" Rodriguez and Craig "Mole" Underhill scored their first kills of Operation Desert Storm. As flight lead of the four-ship that morning, Rodriguez and his wingmen received a pop-up alert from the nearby AWACS. Based on new intel, the four-ship would have to redirect their attention onto several nearby airfields—including H-2, H-3, Mudaysis, Al-Asad, and Al-Taqqadum. "These were the main areas where we knew the Iraqis had fighters."

After an in-flight refueling, Rodriguez hopped back onto the AWACS frequency. The radio traffic was cluttered—fielding calls from F-16s and F-4G Wild Weasels as they prepared to deliver another strike package. "Our new mission," said Rodriguez, "was a pop-up tasking to strike a newly-discovered weapons storage area southwest of Baghdad. The plan was to put 20-30 F-16s onto this target." According to the AWACS, four F-15s would fly in front of the strike formation, conducting a classic pre-strike fighter sweep, while Rico and Mole would fly behind the formation as a "post-strike sweep" to conduct battle damage assessments and engage any lingering MiGs.

"So, as we arrived on the scene," he said, "everything was looking good." But suddenly, the AWACS broke in with an urgent call.

"CITGO 25, pop-up contacts, 40 north of the target area."

Rodriguez had been expecting this. The AWACS call indicated that two unknown aircraft, likely enemy, had been detected approximately forty miles north. "Sure enough, at about 60 miles from us, we picked up two unidentified targets," said Rodriguez. "We were up at 30,000 feet, and we proceeded northeast as we were watching the [F-16s] attacking." As Rodriguez and Underhill vectored to the northeast, both pilots saw the F-16 formation heading south—thus confirming that the F-16s had completed their strike mission.

Just then, however, the trailing F-16 pilot radioed that he had fallen under radar lock from one of the two unidentified aircraft coming from the north. "At this point," Rodriguez said, "we weren't sure what kind of aircraft they were, but they were about 35 miles in trail with the F-16s." The F-16s, however, weren't fazed or even threatened by the lock-on, and continued egressing southward out of the target area—

just in time for Rico and Mole to intercept.

But once their F-15s were within eighteen nautical miles of the incoming bandits, Rodriguez and Underhill were shocked to see both Iraqi planes reverse their course and retreat to the northeast—"back to their base of origin," Rodriguez surmised.

But neither he nor Underhill wanted to let these bandits live to fly another day.

After confirming from the AWACS that there were no other friendlies in the area, Rodriguez and Underhill gave chase to the fleeting bandits. Around this time, both men confirmed that the elusive jets were MiG-29s. "They were quickly moving out of our ability to engage them, as we were in a tail-chase. They were about 12-14 miles off our nose and they had taken it down pretty low; they had pushed it up just about as fast as a MiG-29 could run."

Ironically, the F-15s didn't have to expend as much energy to keep up with these Iraqi MiGs. Although Rodriguez and Underhill were in pursuit at well beyond Mach 1, they did not have to send their engines into full-afterburner to keep pace with the MiG-29. Although these latter-day MiGs were supposedly the pride of the Eastern Bloc air forces, they were still overmatched when pitted against the F-15 Eagle.

While closing in on the Iraqi MiGs, Rodriguez and Underhill realized that they were quickly approaching Baghdad airspace. Within moments, their radar warning systems began to sound the alert of incoming SAMs. Both men were about to clear the airspace when the AWACS interrupted, saying: "CITGO, pop-up targets 330 for 13"— indicating that the bandits were 13 miles away on a heading of 330 degrees. "Out of instinct," said Rodriguez, "I threw my radar into AUTOGUNS and slammed the throttles to full afterburner. I pulled 9-9.5 g's in the turn to put 330 on my nose, and at the same time, reached down and jettisoned my fuel tanks." Craig Underhill followed suit and, within moments, both F-15s gained visual contact of the lead MiG-29.

"At this point, that MiG-29 locks me up,"—Rodriguez's radar system indicated as much. "I execute a defensive maneuver...and dispense a bunch of chaff to break his lock, and cause problems for the MiG-29's radar." Meanwhile, Underhill sprang into action against the leading MiG. Locking onto the leader, Underhill fired an AIM-7.

"Fox 1!" he cried.

Watching the missile glide off Underhill's wing, Rodriguez watched intently as the AIM-7 impacted squarely on its nose, sending the Iraqi bandit into a brilliant flash of molten steel—"literally leaving nothing," said Rodriguez, "and I mean nothing to the imagination other than a big fireball, followed by a large sparkler-like cloud as it descended to the ground." Elated, Rodriguez called "Splash one!" to the AWACS—indicating that Underhill had just destroyed an enemy bandit.

But this was no time to celebrate.

Mere moments after the AWACS confirmed Rodriguez's report, they issued another warning:

"Second bandit, three miles in trail!"

By this point, Rodriguez and Underhill were both at a low altitude, about two and a half miles apart, and the incoming bandit was closing fast to their six o'clock position. Both F-15s executed a hard-right turn to meet the incoming bandit head-on.

But identifying this bandit would be a bit more problematic.

Underhill locked onto the bandit with his radar but couldn't conclusively identify whether this radar signature was friendly or hostile. In the fast-paced, rough-and-tumble world of combat aviation, a fighter pilot has mere seconds to identify an aircraft as "friendly" or "hostile." The pilot must make positive identification—for once he fires a missile, he can never take it back. The ever-present risk of fratricide pressured every pilot to err on the side of caution if he could not identify the bogey from beyond visual range.

Today, as neither Rodriguez nor Underhill could identify the bandit using their onboard instruments, both continued flying forward to visually identify the incoming aircraft. "As the bandit was approaching, we attempt to identify this aircraft from the front aspect...the silhouette and plan form looked a lot like our western fighters, so before we lose an opportunity to maintain an offensive position, I direct the formation to bracket. This set up the VID [visual identification] intercept, which put me in position to run directly on the threat, to get as close as I can to him and try to identify this particular threat. At about a mile and a half, and well below him, I put the bandit on my nose, and I push it up to five stages of burner. As I pass below his left wing by 50-100 feet, I can clearly see the Iraqi paint scheme, his national markings, and that is definitely a MiG-29. I call 'Bandit, Bandit, Bandit.'"

As Rodriguez pulled behind the MiG, its pilot began pulling a slow left turn—seemingly unaware that an American F-15 was moving in behind him. At some point, however, the Iraqi pilot was alerted to Rodriguez's presence, because the MiG soon began to accelerate, vectoring into a defensive turn. Closing in to about 3,000 feet, Rodriguez brought the nose of his aircraft up to align an AIM-7 missile shot.

"I opt to go with the AIM-7," he said, "as we are at a low altitude over the hot desert, and we had seen some problems with the heatseeking AIM-9 [Sidewinder] in this environment." This phenomenon had been a recurring problem with the heatseeking missile. Although heatseeking missiles were a tremendous asset in a dogfight, a pilot had to be careful with how he employed them. As the name implied, the missile would lock on to a target by following the heat from its exhaust manifold. However, the heat-seeking apparatus could easily be fooled by other nearby heat signatures. For instance, if a pilot fired his AIM-9 in the direction of a rising or setting sun, the missile would track onto the sun, and burn out as it chased the solar heat. Likewise, if a pilot fired a heatseeking missile while flying close to the ground (especially a hot desert floor) the missile would nose-dive towards the ground-level heat. Thus, for today's confrontation, Rodriguez selected his radar-tracked AIM-7 Sparrow.

Meanwhile, the Iraqi MiG, perhaps in a state of panic, tried to shake Rodriguez by performing a "Split-S" maneuver. According to Rodriguez, the Split-S was a defensive action wherein an enemy plane rolls upside down, pulls downward, and reverses course—usually as a means to disengage from combat. Rodriguez, however, "wasn't going to take any chances," he said. "So, I rolled hard off his tail and climbed it up to the vertical. I then rolled to look down and reacquire a tally on the bandit. I then witness the bandit impact the ground."

Indeed, while attempting to evade Rodriguez, the Iraqi pilot had inadvertently plummeted himself into the ground. "As he hit the desert floor," Rodriguez continued, "he hadn't quite gotten perpendicular to the ground. I could clearly see his afterburners cooking, and his stabs were dug in…and the wreckage continues to create a fireball for miles across the desert."

Reflecting on the engagement, Rodriguez commented that "through hard training and solid squadron standards between flight leads and wingmen, Mole and I were able to successfully complete this piece of the mission, with surprisingly little comm. We knew what each of us was doing."

Chapter 5

FIRE AND FURY

After merely three days into the air war, the IQAF was in full panic. On the ground and in the air, the pride of Saddam's air force was being decimated by the Allied air offensive. "If we didn't have air superiority before January 19," said Rick Tollini, "we definitely had established it after." Indeed, during the first 48 hours, the IQAF had thrown its best fighters against the coalition air forces…and paid dearly for it.

Oddly enough, after January 19, the Iraqi Air Force stood down for nearly a week; they didn't generate a single combat sortie.

"Nothing flew," said Tollini. "Not a thing."

But Tollini had his own theory behind the unexpected lull in combat operations: "It may seem that to lose four or five jet fighters in a day (among the hundreds of frontline fighters available to the Iraqis) would not be a big deal, but in modern warfare I believe it's different. It is more about the way it happens and the impact on the psyche of the pilots, squadrons, and command elements involved. When you throw your best pilots and best game plan out there, and it doesn't even come close to being successful, the morale of a unit and an air force can be destroyed."

Still, the 58th Fighter Squadron stayed on the forefront of the Allied air campaign—flying DCA, OCA, and escort missions. "And the 18-hour duty cycle became exhausting," Tollini added. "After two weeks most of us were walking around like zombies." The steady intake of "Go" and "No-Go" pills, however, were enough to regulate their vital functions.

Although the Iraqi MiGs and Mirages had disappeared for the moment, it seemed that the squadron's escort missions had become more dangerous than dogfighting. Mark Arriola, for example, had a near-death experience while escorting a strike force of twenty-four F-111s. "Their target was one of Saddam's presidential palaces southeast of Baghdad. Intel reported that Saddam was there, and these guys were going to go level the place." While flying on Chuck Magill's wing that night, Mark recalled that the weather was exceptionally bad. "There were a *ton* of thunderstorms that night," he said. "And we were actually refueling among the thunderstorms." Indeed, it was terrifying to see streaks of lightning pass within a few hundred feet of their cockpits. He later remarked that he was more afraid of getting fuel that night than he was of flying into combat.

"We were supposed to have a flight of [F-4] Wild Weasels with us," said Mark, "who would knock out the Iraqi SAM radars if they tried to lock us up. But those guys [F-4s] got delayed because of the weather." The F-111s, however, insisted on pushing through with the original start time. But without the Wild Weasels' suppression of enemy air defenses, the F-111s and F-15s would have no shield against the incoming SAMs.

These F-111s, meanwhile, were carrying 2,000-lb bombs which, as Arriola remembered, added considerably to the planes' time over target. Given the ballistics of the 2,000-lb bombs, the shrapnel from each bomb had to settle over the target area before the next F-111 could drop its proceeding ordnance. Taken together, it was a "30-40-minute time-over-target window," said Mark. As the escort team, the F-15s had to circle the area while the F-111s initiated their bombing runs. "Well, during that time," he said, "we were kind of like sitting ducks up there because we're not really moving in space, we're just staying in the same general piece of sky."

Suddenly, Mark's radar warning receiver sounded an alert.

The Iraqi SAMs had locked onto the F-15s.

"At first, they were trying to lock us up with their target tracking systems," Arriola continued. But by this point in the air war, the Iraqis knew that turning on their radar trackers would draw attention from the F-4 Wild Weasels. Fortunately, the Iraqis didn't know that the F-4s had been grounded due to weather. Still, the SAM batteries had obviously anticipated the F-4s' arrival because the Iraqis soon turned off their radars and began firing their missiles ballistically. "And there were so many of them," added Mark, "that their chances of hitting us were more than 50/50."

Mark's flight leader, Chuck Magill, yelled "Break Now! Break Now!"—calling for evasive maneuvers. "So, I rolled and inverted," said Mark, "and jettisoned my external fuel tanks." But as Mark rolled into the turn, the proximity fuse from an SA-3 missile hit one of his descending fuel tanks. Luckily, the falling tank had gained some distance between itself and the plane before hitting the SA-3, but not enough to shield Arriola's F-15 from the resulting shock wave. "My helmet went into the canopy and it cracked my helmet."

Dazed from the explosion, Mark regained his senses just in time to see his F-15 hurtling towards the ground at more than 500 knots. When the initial explosion rocked his plane, he had been at 30,000 feet. But by the time he pulled his plane out of the nosedive he was barely 800 feet off the ground. "And the next thing you know, I see all this AAA coming up, and I throw it into full afterburner and start climbing." He quickly reestablished contact with Magill and the rest of the flight as they regrouped from the hasty SAM break.

By now the F-111 strike package was preparing to egress. "As we started climbing back up to cover the last F-111," said Mark, "we got a call from the AWACS saying that we have an inbound bogey." Locking on to the mysterious bogey, Chuck Magill began to ping it with the electronic query of the AAI.

But Magill didn't get a "friendly" reply from the inbound aircraft.

Fearing that this bogey may have been a wayward MiG, the entire flight of F-15s directed their attention onto the incoming plane. Moments later, however, the AWACS broke in, yelling:

"Friendly! Friendly! Friendly!"

It was another F-111 that had just come off target, but missed its egress point, and was now struggling to catch up with the rest of the formation. "That just goes to show you how disciplined we were," said Arriola, "with our rules of engagement—when we could fire, when we couldn't fire." Indeed, a lesser-trained pilot would have opened fire on the F-111 after the first negative AAI response.

The following day, January 21, Mark Arriola and Chuck Magill were flying a two-ship HVAA escort when they received a mayday call from a downed F-14 Tomcat. Earlier that morning, US Navy Lieutenant Devon Jones and his Radar Intercept Officer (RIO), Lieutenant Lawrence Slade, had taken flight from the USS Saratoga aboard an F-14 call-signed SLATE 46. As part of a fighter escort mission targeting the Mudaysis Air Base, SLATE 46 was barely over the target area when Jones spied a surface-to-air missile rising from the clouds. ""My RIO [Slade] saw it, too. It turned out to be an old SA-2, like the ones used in Vietnam."

Instinctively, Jones took the F-14 into evasive action.

"I added power, rolled into the SAM…to give the missile tracking problems." Sadly, his evasive maneuver wasn't fast enough. As Jones rolled the Tomcat downward, the missile tracked him, coming up towards the tail of SLATE 46, detonating in a flash of blinding light. The Tomcat shuddered violently, but kept rolling to the right. Unbeknownst to Jones and Slade, the aircraft's tail had just been severed.

Both men ejected safely, but their parachutes drifted away from one another. Jones' wingman, however, had seen the F-14 go down, and made an obligatory distress call. Slade had likewise made a distress call from his PRC-112 radio during the parachute descent. By now, the carrier group knew that one of their own had been shot down. Soon, all coalition aircraft in the area would be advised of the same.

As Jones touched down on the desert floor, he began making his own mayday calls from his UHF radio. At about 12:00 noon, Chuck Magill intercepted one of the calls. "And so Chuck and I are talking to this guy on UHF," said Mark, "trying to get an actual location." If Magill and Arriola could pinpoint his whereabouts, they could vector a Search and Rescue (SAR) team onto his location. Unfortunately for Jones, he had landed near the vicinity of Mudaysis proper. "The Brits had pretty much decimated the runway at Mudaysis," said Arriola, "so there weren't any aircraft there… but there were a lot of Republican Guardsmen." Unlike the Iraqi regulars, most of whom were poorly-trained and poorly-led conscripts, the Republican Guard were Iraq's elite ground forces. They were the best-equipped of Iraq's troops and they were fiercely loyal to Saddam.

Descending to about 18,000 feet, Magill spoke with Jones over the radio just as Arriola spied a column of Iraqi trucks filing out of Mudaysis…all of which were barreling straight towards Jones' location. It was then that Jones, Magill, and Arriolla realized that the Iraqis had been listening to the unsecured UHF frequency, and had used the radio traffic to pinpoint Jones' location. "So we stopped him from making any more radio calls," said Arriola, "and Sly gets on the horn talking to the AWACS." Magill made a frantic plea to the AWACS to scramble any nearby attack aircraft—a downed aviator was about to be captured, and the incoming column had to be strafed and destroyed. Although their own F-15s weren't the most-suitable aircraft for air-to-ground missions, both men were prepared to strafe the column as best they could if no other aircraft could support. Luckily, the AWACS got ahold of a nearby flight of A-10 Warthogs, who happily answered the call to strafe and level the incoming Iraqis.

Magill, acting as a forward air controller, directed the A-10s onto Jones' location. Admittedly, Lieutenant Jones was panicking, but his panic turned to relief when he saw the 30mm guns from the A-10s make short work of the lead Iraqi vehicle. Indeed, after a few strafing runs, the A-10s had left nothing but flames and dust of the Iraqi troops. By the time the lead Iraqi truck plodded to a fiery halt, it was barely 100 yards from Jones's hiding spot.

From Mark Arriola's position, he saw the lead A-10 get a tally on the convoy, strafing the column and delivering a massive cluster bomb. Somewhat amused, Arriola noted that the Republican Guardsmen "scattered in every cardinal direction, running for the desert." By this time, the second A-10 had descended onto the column, firing his Maverick missile, and destroying the lead truck as it ambled closer to Jones' position. For the next few minutes, the pair of A-10s cycled through the column—"and they just decimated this convoy of troops and trucks," said Arriola.

A few moments later, a team of Air Force heliborne commandos arrived to take Jones back to the *Saratoga*. The lead helicopter touched down about twenty yards from Jones's spider hole. "One of the special forces guys jumped out and waved me on," he recalled. "I jumped in and off we went, 140 miles to go at 140 knots." He had spent eight hours behind enemy lines. Returning to his squadron, Jones was eternally grateful to the Air Force commandos who had risked their lives to save his own. "Big spines on these guys, I'll tell you, being 150 miles into enemy territory during the day."

His RIO, Lieutenant Slade, however, hadn't been so lucky. He was captured earlier that morning and spent the remainder of the war in a Baghdad prison alongside other downed coalition aviators, including a pair of British Tornado pilots. Slade was released from captivity on March 4, 1991.

By January 26, the Iraqi Air Force seemed to be catching its second wind. One week after their unexpected standdown, wherein no Iraqi planes had taken flight, the IQAF suddenly began generating more sorties. That morning of the 26th, Rico Rodriguez achieved his second kill of Desert Storm—this time against a MiG-23 Flogger. Among the Soviet-built fighters, the MiG-23 and its variants were among the most derided. Although its "swing wing" design was revolutionary for its time, the aircraft was an exceptionally poor dogfighter. The Israeli and Iranian pilots whom had flown against the MiG-23 were unanimous in their disdain for it. As one US Marine pilot recalled: "The MiG-23 was a maneuvering 'dog.' Even the F-4 Phantom could out-turn it." Thus, it came as no surprise that the MiG-23 was easy prey for coalition fighters.

On this morning of January 26, as the Iraqi Air Force was struggling to survive, Rodriguez was more concerned about the weather. Poor weather conditions had already grounded much of the coalition's aircraft. Of the few aircraft that did take flight that day, most were DCA missions—in this case, roaming air patrols looking for targets of opportunity and/or keeping the skies clear for friendly reconnaissance flights.

With Bruce Till on his wing, Rodriguez manned the Number 3 position of a four-ship flight led by Rhory Draeger. Draeger's wingman was Tony "Kimo" Schiavi. Rodriguez's normal wingman, Craig Underhill, was back at the airbase, completing his turn for the rotational "squadron supervisor" position.

Although the war was now into its second week, today's sortie had been relatively quiet. The AWACS had called in a few contact reports—most of which turned out to be false alarms. Rodriguez and his wingmen continued along their flight path until the AWACS interrupted once again. This time, the controller reported aircraft activity farther west near the H-2 and H-3 airfields.

Acknowledging the call, the four-ship headed southwest, maintaining their altitude above 30,000 feet to conserve fuel and stay above the cloud deck. "At about 80 miles," said Rico, "AWACS informs us that there are aircraft taking off, and as we approached 70 miles, we also get radar contact. Thanks to some fantastic support from the AWACS, we were informed that these were MiG-23s before we even had a chance to lock up the contacts." As the formation proceeded to merge with the enemy bandits, Rodriguez noticed that, based on his map, these MiGs appeared to be following a major highway northeast towards Baghdad. "Our post-flight speculation," he said, "was that once these aircraft landed, they would refuel and attempt to run to Iran." Indeed, this second week of the air campaign marked the beginning of a "mass exodus" of Iraqi aircraft to Iran. Wanting to preserve what was left of their air force, several Iraqi units began flying their jets into Iran, hoping to use the shield of Iranian neutrality as a means to wait out the conflict.

"The clouds were still pretty thick," Rodriguez continued. "So, we didn't think that we were going to see the missiles do their job, but at forty miles the clouds started to break, and we could see all the way to the ground." This was fortuitous, as the F-15s could now identify the MiG-23s visually, without the use of avionics. "In the F-15, firepower is awesome," said Tony Schiavi. "When you get four F-15s running in a wall towards somebody, there's no way you're not going to come out victorious." And these MiG-23s were about to experience the Eagles' firepower firsthand.

"Rhory collapsed the formation so we could get through a hole in the clouds in our descent," Rodriguez continued. "Once underneath, at about 15,000 feet he spread the formation back out into the wall, and that's when the enemy formation became clear. The MiG-23s were in a 'Vic' formation [Flying-V], with the leader on the point, and the two wingmen space aft on a 45-degree line on each side [three MiGs in total]. There was a two-mile space between the leader and the other two as they navigated along the highway."

Accelerating to merge with the MiGs, Draeger went after the leader, Schiavi went after the northern wingman, while Till and Rodriguez targeted the southern. Draeger fired first, launching an AIM-7 into the lead MiG. Although the missile catapulted squarely into the MiGs fuselage, it surprisingly did not detonate. Instead, the missile ripped through the intake manifold, shattering the MiG's engine. The ailing bandit careened to its left before the shattered engine caught fire, engulfing the pilot in flames.

"As the missiles start flying off," said Tony Schiavi, "we pick up the first tally-hos about ten miles from the merge," meaning the four-ship had visual ID of the bandits at a distance of ten miles. "We can see the Floggers running across the desert, fast. A lot of times you can see the missile, and you can keep a tally-ho on that missile." While admiring Drager's handiwork against the leading MiG, however, Schiavi had nearly forgotten about his own missile. "Right about then, my missile hits my guy. I call a second 'splash.'" It was Tony Schiavi's first kill of Desert Storm.

Till and Rodriguez, meanwhile, fired their AIM-7 missiles almost simultaneously at the third, southernmost MiG. Luckily for Rico, his missile landed first—sending the MiG hurtling into the desert floor and confirming his second kill of Desert Storm.

"None of the MiG pilots managed to eject," said Rodriguez.

"As for what the MiGs looked like," Schiavi added, "they were camo'd, and they were about two-and-a-half to three miles in front of us when they actually blew up, so we saw them pretty well." Draeger, meanwhile, reappeared on the radio:

"Let's come off north," he said, directing the four-ship flight to vacate the area.

"First thing you do when you start blowing guys up," said Tony Schiavi, "is you think about getting the hell out of there, fast. Once people [i.e., the enemy] see fireballs, that gets their attention, and you don't want to be around."

Rodriguez later recalled that he and Draeger were the only two pilots in the four-ship who had gotten previous MiG kills. "The prior experience helped us stay calm," he admitted, "and our wingmen perceived this, and it helped them execute very well in their first engagement."

Between many of these sorties, Chief Matos and his crews often had to change the F-15s' tires. The tires on the landing gear were rated for only so many landings...and the desert heat certainly added to their wear and tear. "But changing tires on the F-15 was very simple," he said. "On the F-4 Phantom, it was a son of a bitch!"

As the coalition continued bombing Iraqi airfields, more and more IQAF planes began fleeing to Iran. "They probably figured it was better to run for it than to lose most of their modern aircraft as they sat on the ground," surmised Rick Tollini.

But these refugee flights into Iran had become a top news story.

CNN correspondents started asking: "Where were our Coalition fighters? And why were we letting the Iraqi fighters escape?" Valid questions, but Tollini disliked the word "escape."

"Hell," he said, "they were just trying to save their ass."

"I figured the more [planes] that went to Iran and Syria the better, because they were never going to come back, and it might just end this war sooner than later."

CENTAF, however, disagreed.

They subsequently established a network of CAP stations along the Iranian border to intercept any fleeting Iraqi aircraft. The 58th Fighter Squadron thus found itself assigned to the so-called "CINDY CAP"—a combat air patrol station that someone at CENTAF had arbitrarily named CINDY (perhaps the namesake of a wife or daughter).

But flying these CAPs along the Iranian border was a "huge undertaking," said Bill Thiel. "You had to have two CAPs along the border in 8-10-hour shifts." And because the tankers were all south of the Saudi border, the F-15s would have to fly across the biggest swaths of Iraqi airspace just to reach the refuel point. The real problem with the CINDY CAP station, however, was its location. "It was a small piece of airspace that was nestled just outside the Eastern Missile Engagement Zone of Baghdad, right along the Iranian border," said Mark Arriola. "And it was severely mountainous terrain. The closest divert was Diyarbakir, Turkey…and it was an hour and a half away." For every round-trip to the CINDY CAP, "you had to circumnavigate quite a number of Missile Engagement Zones," he continued. "And if you didn't pay attention, you'd be in a lethality ring over Baghdad…and the chances of them getting you with a surface-to-air missile were pretty high. Occasionally, we'd also get sampled by Iranian Tomcats [from across the border], but they never pressed an engagement."

The CINDY CAP itself was only about 30 miles wide, but it was the closest aerial corridor between Baghdad and the Iranian border. CENTAF, therefore, determined that this would be the most likely avenue of approach taken by the refugee bandits. But the CINDY CAP station was never effective because the Iraqis knew the F-15s were there. The fleeting bandits just found other places to cross the border, while Iraqi ground units repositioned their SAM batteries to fire on the F-15s circling above.

"We were lucky we never lost an Eagle there," said Rick Tollini, "but a Langley [1st Fighter Wing] jet almost got hit one night right after I had transferred control to them. I alerted them that AWACS had warned us of an enemy height-finder radar active in the area, a sure-fire hint they were about ready to launch something. The Iraqis wanted to know the altitude of our fighters, and sure enough they did. Fight a war for long enough, and people (mostly generals and politicians) will start coming up with stupid things to do. The CINDY CAP was the best example for us…I told our pilots not to CAP or orbit there, but just to pass through the region momentarily and then go on to other areas along the border in a random fashion. Once we started doing this, the Iraqis never knew exactly where we were going to be or where we were going next. So, occasionally we were able to catch some Iraqi fighters by surprise as they tried to get out of town."

On January 29, 1991—the first day of the dreaded CINDY CAP mission—Captain David "Logger" Rose downed an Iraqi MiG-23 near the Iranian border. "We had not been up north of Baghdad yet, so it was pretty interesting to get to go up there and check out a new area of the country," he said. "There is a huge lake just northwest of Baghdad, and there was a ton of smoke coming off the refineries and targets that were still on fire. The weather was also different on this day…as there was a broken overcast at about 18-20,000 feet. It was either go high and stay above it or go below, and we decided to go below. This way we could see any SAMs as they came up, and also, that far north, AWACS couldn't see much, and even less down low."

As Rose and his wingman, Kevin "Coppertone" Gallagher, settled into their CAP station, both men marveled at the terrain below. Unlike most of Iraq, which was a flat and barren desert, the Iranian borderlands were quite mountainous. "It was pretty," said Rose, "and you could definitely see the border where, during the years of their conflict [Iran-Iraq War], they had built barricades, trenches, and emplacements along the border. That was interesting to look at, as we were CAPing basically east-west."

Suddenly, Gallagher noticed a radar contact—a low-flying, fast-moving bogey eastbound at fifty miles. Moments later, Rose picked up the same contact. But he noticed something peculiar about its flight pattern: "He is down low, and doing about 720 knots right on the deck at about 300 feet"—not the typical flight characteristics for an Iraqi MiG unless they were trying to escape and avoid detection. "I call it out to the AWACS, who doesn't see the contact, but does pass that there are friendlies in the area. Now we know we've got to do an intercept." Indeed, because there were other Allied aircraft in the vicinity, Rose knew he couldn't shoot from beyond visual range due to the high probability of fratricide. "This meant our intercept would need to put us behind the contact so we could visually confirm that they were hostile types before engaging them. So we pushed it up, and we were at about 16,000 feet because of the overcast, doing about 650 knots."

At about fifteen miles out, Rose got radar lock on the bandit, and jettisoned his fuel tanks to pick up speed. At first, he saw no other radar contacts, indicating that this fleeting bandit was alone. "I rolled in from about 15,000 feet down to about 8,000 feet, two-and-a-half miles behind a brown-on-brown Flogger"—a MiG-23 sporting the typical IQAF camo scheme. "I had an AIM-9 tone on the bandit," Rose continued, "but I chose to shoot an AIM-7 radar-guided missile, just because it's a bigger warhead. This was the first time I had shot an AIM-7, and felt the 'thunk' as it came off, and I saw the smoke trail."

A mere ten seconds later, the AIM-7 detonated right on the spine of the Flogger, hurtling the fiery carcass of the Iraqi MiG onto the desert floor.

"Splash One!" he cried.

But his wingman, Coppertone Gallagher, wasn't done yet.

"He had gotten contact on a second bandit," Rose recalled. The lone bandit that Rose had just killed hadn't been alone after all. "Coppertone has this guy locked up at about 3.5 miles in front of me, and I lock up this second Flogger also," Rose continued. "By this time, we're getting into the foothills, and the bandit is having to climb up over those, so he's a little easier to see."

At about this time, Gallagher fired an AIM-7. But as the missile trailed off towards the fleeting bandit, something else caught Rose's attention.

From the corner of his eye, he saw another F-15 suddenly appear off Gallagher's wing.

"Who the heck is this guy?" Rose wondered.

He wasn't one of their wingmen, and his tail markings didn't match any of the Eglin units.

But whoever this stranger may have been, he had now joined the pursuit, and was taking aim at the Iraqi Flogger. "This other Eagle also shoots an AIM-7 at this bandit," but Gallagher wasn't ready to yield the pursuit; he fired a second AIM-7 almost in unison with his newfound wingman. "Coppertone's missile detonates to the right of the bandit," said Rose, "but [the MiG] keeps on flying." The missile from the other Eagle, however, drifted into the ground.

By now, this second bandit was inching closer to the border, and had somehow dodged two AIM-7s. Not wanting the second MiG to get away, Rose climbed up and fired another Sparrow.

"I wait and wait, but there is no fireball."

But as the AIM-7 was getting closer and closer to timing out, Rose and Gallagher were getting closer and closer to Iranian airspace. Moreover, they were running low on fuel. "The bandit is having to climb now, since the hills are turning into mountains; and there is no fireball, so I had no idea what happened to my missile. But after three shots, this was one lucky enemy fighter!" Indeed, this wayward MiG escaped three AIM-7 missiles and made it safely across the Iranian border. But the fact remained that David "Logger" Rose had downed an enemy bandit, earning the squadron its thirteenth kill of the air war.

"We get back to Tabuk," he said, "and the tradition was that if you had a victory, you did an aileron roll coming up initial." But by now, it was dark, and a full moon had risen over the desert landscape. Typically, fliers were discouraged from doing the aileron roll while landing at night, but Rose did it anyway. "I pulled close and came back around and landed, and the Wing Commander [Colonel Parsons] met me at the jet."

At first, Rose thought he was in serious trouble.

Parsons was a competent commander, but he had varying degrees of tolerance for the garden-variety antics of his "fighter jocks." Luckily for Rose, Colonel Parsons was only there to congratulate him for being in the right place at the right time.

He later discovered that the strange Eagle who had appeared off Gallagher's wing belonged to the F-15 squadrons operating from Incirlik Air Base in Turkey. As it turned out, a northern AWACS had vectored the Incirlik Eagle and his wingman onto the same bandits Rose and Gallagher were already chasing. "Neither of them knew we were there until my missile blew up the first MiG," said Rose. Luckily, their onboard AAIs had prevented any incidents of fratricide that day.

It was also during one of the border reconnaissance flights when, on February 7, 1991, Tony Murphy intercepted a pair of Iraqi Su-22s. "The squadron had 13 kills already," he said, and it looked as though the IQAF was running out of planes to send aloft. Still, his job was to keep the enemy fighters from reaching Iran.

By the first week of February, the 58th Fighter Squadron had established a recurring patrol pattern along the Iranian border. Because Murphy's regular wingman had returned to the US on a family emergency, the squadron had rendered Murphy a "pick-up pilot" of sorts—filling in for other pilots and missions on an as-needed basis. On this day, Colonel Rick Parsons, the wing commander, was leading a two-ship flight to the Iranian border. Thus, Murphy was tasked to be his wingman. Until now, most of the sorties had been four-plane formations but because this had been a short-alert tasking, it was only Parsons and Murphy who were going aloft. Such pairings between a junior and senior officer were not uncommon. "We had flown together occasionally," said Murphy, "so this was not our first sortie together."

Early that morning, "I went in an hour before the briefing to find out who my tankers were, where they were going to be, and what freqs [frequencies] they were going to be on," said Murphy. "Then I checked on who the AWACS controllers were, and what freqs they used, and where they were going to be so I could look at their radar coverage. They sometimes got so far away that we couldn't talk to them or they couldn't see beyond us." When Colonel Parsons arrived for the briefing, "we went through the new threats and assigned responsibilities." Each man had to be on the lookout for any late-model Iraqi MiGs or tactical Sukhois. The fighter fleet was the supposed "crown jewel" of the IQAF, and they had priority clearance to fly into Iran as a means to escape the Allied onslaught.

"We launched and headed for the Iranian border. We had to fly about an hour and 15 minutes to get on station and hit a tanker early because it's nice to have lots of gas," said Murphy. "From there, we wanted to go due north on the east side of Baghdad to avoid all the SAM sites around the city. Our standard load-out was three bags of gas and four each of AIM-7s and AIM-9s, plus the gun. Our plan was to get past the SAMs and patrol in a north-south pattern, versus the usual east-west. We had just passed north of Baghdad when my wingman [Parsons] called out a radar contact. I moved my radar up and saw the same. AWACS confirmed that we were the only friendly aircraft in the area, so it was starting to firm up in my mind that these were hostile groups."

Murphy started the intercept by vectoring east, targeting the group leader. After verifying the range to target, Murphy locked onto the first bandit and fired an AIM-7. "My missile comes off and appears to be tracking to the target." But as Murphy brought up the nose of his aircraft, hoping to center the bandit on his Heads-Up Display (HUD), he noticed a brilliant flash, followed by the sight of the Su-22 rolling in the dirt.

Setting his sights onto the second bandit, Murphy locked onto the fleeting Sukhoi and fired another AIM-7. "Right then," he recalled, "the AWACS calls that the border is 15 miles on our nose"—meaning that Murphy was only a few moments away from violating Iranian airspace. Murphy jinked his F-15 southward, taking the momentum of the turn to put more airspace between himself and the border; and he recovered just in time to see his second missile lose its lock on the bandit. Undeterred, Murphy fired yet another AIM-7...downing the second Su-22 with a solid hit just behind the canopy.

"This is when I realize two things," he said.

"First, is that the distance from his aircraft to his shadow was the same as his wingspan! So he's about 50 feet [in altitude]. Second, this is the first time I realize that I'm at only 100 feet! It shows you how focused you can get on the target."

Although he was certain that his target had been an Su-22, or perhaps an early-generation MiG, it was not until later that Air Intelligence confirmed his kills to be Su-22s. The Sukhoi Su-22 had been a frequent visitor to American air patrols in and around the Middle East. In 1981, for example, two Libyan Su-22s had engaged a pair of F-14 Tomcats over the Gulf of Sidra...with both Sukhois promptly being destroyed by the American Tomcats.

Today's brief dogfight had been no different.

Both Su-22s plummeted to the Earth—victims of the AIM-7 missile.

As Murphy pulled up from the engagement, he spied another Iraqi aircraft in flames, hurtling towards the ground. As it turned out Colonel Parsons had just downed a Sukhoi Su-7—another fighter of similar vintage to the MiG-21.

Low on fuel, Murphy and Parsons decided to head home. "We were 200 to 250 miles from the tankers on the other side of the border and 600 miles from home," Murphy recalled. "We climbed to 46,000 feet and slowed down to conserve gas while I tried to get a tanker as far north as they would go. A KC-10 gave us gas rather promptly, so I began feeling a lot better with that full load of fuel." Murphy then radioed to the AWACS that he and Colonel Parsons were returning to base.

"Wait a minute," the AWACS replied. "You're supposed to be here for six hours and you've only been here for two. What's going on?"

"We've got no ordnance," Murphy replied, "or external tanks, so we're going home."

AWACS rogered the call and scrambled another flight of F-15s to the area that Murphy and Parsons had just vacated.

At fifty miles out, ET Murphy and Colonel Parsons began fielding their standard calls to the maintenance crews: how many missiles they had fired, how many fuel tanks they had dropped, and the serviceability codes of both airframes. "When I called that I had shot four missiles, they figured something had happened. By the time we got home, there were 150 people on the ramp," he said— practically the entire American contingent at Tabuk, each of whom were eager to hear about Murphy's and Parson's latter-day kills. By this point in the air war, few pilots (if any) had expected to see any more Iraqi aircraft. But news of the double kill travelled quickly, and the squadron members were eager to hear about it.

"I flew the traditional two victory rolls for my kills,

landed, and taxied up to the ramp," Murphy continued. "Everybody congratulated us and asked all kinds of questions. Colonel Parsons and I made our report to the command section in Riyadh," and were soon met by a reporter from *Airman Magazine.* "I filed a claim that day for two kills," said Murphy, "and confirmed Colonel Parsons' kill."

Said Colonel Parsons of the engagement: "These were the last three kills credited to the [58th Fighter Squadron, 33d Fighter Wing], bringing the total to sixteen, the most of any unit in Desert Storm. There should be no doubt that superior machines, realistic training, and top-notch freedom-loving supporters, maintainers, and jocks make an unbeatable force. Of those wing members who stayed behind [at Eglin], all wanted to be in on the action. Their support, and that of all our families, contributed incalculably to the success of those deployed."

Meanwhile, back at Eglin, Colonel Rich Hardy continued to keep the families updated on the happenings of their loved ones in the Gulf. "I would hold meetings occasionally to talk to the wives and I let them know what I could." These meetings, however, could be heart-rending sessions, especially after the air war began. "These young people," said Hardy, "had never experienced anything like this"—the separation of war and the anxiety of having a spouse deployed to a combat zone. "We had babies being born to fathers who were deployed; and the mothers at home weren't too happy."

Still, Hardy did his best to support the families at Eglin. "We had a lot of volunteers," he said—many of whom dropped off groceries, carpooled, offered child care services, or helped with household chores.

After the air war kicked off, Rich Hardy also bore the task of informing the wives that their husbands had achieved the USAF's first air-to-air victories since Vietnam. Cesar

Rodriguez's wife Trish, for example, was both stunned and elated to hear of her husband's multiple MiG kills. Of course, none of the spouses were happy to hear that people were dying. But this was war. And the wives were glad that their husbands were fighting valiantly and, moreover, that they were surviving. "Killing is obviously not something you want your husband to do," said Christine Murphy, "but then again, the Iraqi planes were a threat to our forces, so we were just as obviously glad our guys won. It's easy to deny the really serious part of the fighter profession because they spend many years training for something that may never happen. Many guys train for years and never see combat."

"Endless hours over the barren desert, in a combat-loaded Eagle, and guys start looking for something, anything, to shoot at," said Rick Tollini. Such was the case when Rob "Cheese" Graeter and his wingman Scott "Papa" Maw were flying OCA near Mudaysis. "The F-15 radar is so good that it can sometimes lock-up vehicles on the highway, if they are traveling fast enough." On this day, Maw and Graeter picked up a low-lying radar contact which they assumed to be an Iraqi helicopter. By the time they arrived on station, however, they were disappointed to see that it was just an Iraqi Army truck. But when the occupants of said truck spied two incoming F-15s, the panicked Iraqis quickly pulled off to the side of the road and ran for cover into a nearby ditch.

Graeter, who was leading the flight that day, reported his observation to the AWACS, who then confirmed that the fleeting truck and troops were a valid target—"so why not strafe it with the Eagle's 20mm cannon?" The only problem was…neither Scott Maw nor Rob Graeter had ever strafed a ground target before.

Still, that didn't stop either pilot from trying to flex his ground-attack skills.

"On each attempt," Tollini recalled, "Cheese and Papa would miss, and miss so badly, that the poor Iraqi military occupants hiding in the ditch likely feared for their lives. Cheese said that every time he and Papa completed another pass, Cheese would see the Iraqis get up and scramble to another ditch farther away." After many unsuccessful attempts, Maw and Graeter finally succeeded in strafing the truck.

"What they got for their effort, though, was grounded."

Indeed, when Colonel Parsons learned of the strafing, he grounded both pilots for nearly a week.

As expected, Parsons' decision was wildly unpopular.

"Cheese was one of our most experienced mission commanders and weapons officers," Tollini protested, "and we needed him in the air." Colonel Parsons ordered no further strafing missions unless specifically directed by the Airborne Combat Element (ACE) aboard the AWACS. But a few days later, Rick Tollini was flying a midday area-denial mission when the AWACS came over the radio with such a call.

That day, "I decided to take the 4-ship across the area just north of Baghdad, head toward the Iranian border, and then head back around Baghdad in a counter-clockwise flow to join up with our airborne tanker," Tollini said. "About the only action we got most of the day was some random large-caliber AAA coming up to around 25,000 feet and leaving sizeable black clouds of shrapnel patterns in the sky."

As the formation headed east, however, one of the wingmen spotted a large Iraqi transport aircraft standing alone on an airfield just northeast of Baghdad. "I decided to drop down a little closer and use my Eagle Eye rifle scope to get a closer look at the airplane."

Sure enough, the mystery transport was a Soviet-built Ilyushin IL-76 "Candid."

Tollini described it as a medium cargo carrier, similar to a Lockheed C-141 Starlifter. "The Candid had been parked on a ramp, and it had a circle of sandbags or some other kind of temporary barrier built up around it," he continued. "That alone made it look like an important target. We had been told at the start of the war to be on the lookout for these large-type cargo aircraft. They would be what Saddam would likely use if he decided to leave the country. The Iraqis had also been known to load chemical weapons on these aircraft and use them as toxic 'crop dusters' to spray extensive areas with deadly chemicals like Sarin nerve gas."

Naturally, the IL-76 was considered a high-priority target.

"I reported the sighting to our AWACS controller," and requested scrambling any nearby F-16s to strafe the lone Candid. "I would hold our 4-ship on station to help protect the strike aircraft," he added. AWACS acknowledged the call, and relayed that he would scramble Vipers in the air at the earliest availability. "So, we went on about our business," Tollini continued, "and eventually returned to our tanker for a refueling. It was about an hour or two later that we were back up in the same area again, and as we flew by the airfield we saw the same IL-76 on the ground, apparently untouched."

Tollini again asked if any F-16s could be vectored to strafe the target. AWACS replied that none were available, but followed up with: "Can your flight strafe it?" Remembering Colonel Parsons admonition, Tollini came back with:

"Ummm, well, we are not allowed to strafe unless the ACE directs us to strafe."

Tollini expected that to be the end of the conversation,

until he heard the AWACS say:

"Roger. ACE directs you strafe the Candid."

"Copy! Cleared to strafe!"

Flying in Tollini's formation that day was Captain Steve "Mongo" Robbins—one of his former Weapons School mentors. "He had been sent to Saudi Arabia with the task of gathering all the information he could about the air war—our results and lessons learned—and compile an extensive 'Baron' report, or after-action report," said Tollini. "Flying with the best unit in the theater was going to help him do it, and I could not help but feel a sense of pride that Mongo would be flying as #3 in my 4-ship on this day."

At that point, Tollini split his four-ship flight into two elements. "This was Mongo's chance to get into the war and get some ordnance off of his jet...so I told him to go in hot and take #4 (ET Murphy) with him." Meanwhile, Cherry Pitts and Tollini would stay up high as "top cover." During a strafing run, it was good practice to have another set of aircraft covering the area to ward off any lingering MiGs and watch for enemy SAMs.

Pitts and Tollini watched as Mongo Robbins rolled in, executing a near-perfect strafing run. "With cautionary defensive chaff and flares spewing from his Eagle, he got a perfect hit on the Candid's right wing, which exploded into a little ball of fire. Mongo would later relate to us back at Tabuk that as he sighted up the target, he noticed a bunch of people sitting near the Candid. Apparently, they saw Mongo pointing his Eagle right at them, and Mongo watched as, he said, they scattered like a bunch of ants surprised at a summer picnic."

Although the F-15C wasn't optimized for air-to-ground operations, Tollini had already figured out how to adapt the plane for ground attack sorties. One of his earlier mentors in the 12th Fighter Squadron at Kadena Air Base had previously flown A-7 Corsair attack planes. According to the old mentor, the gunsight positions on the A-7 and F-15C were identical. Thus, if an air-superiority F-15 ever had to strafe, the pilot need only adjust the radar for ranging to the ground, dial the gun reticle to 30-mils depression, dive shallow at 20 degrees nose-low, and hit the trigger at 6,000 feet "slant range." Tollini had actually practiced this technique back at Eglin while training for the William Tell Competition.

This morning, he had briefed the four-ship flight on how to use this very technique, but he never expected to use it in combat. Going into Desert Storm, every bit of intel suggested they'd have plenty of MiGs to keep them busy. Air-to-ground operations were, after all, the province of Strike Eagles, Warthogs, Wild Weasels, and F-111s.

As the coalition established (and maintained) air superiority over Iraq, Rick Tollini's time in the 58th Fighter Squadron was growing short. Since the previous summer, he had been on orders to return to the 12th Fighter Squadron in Okinawa. The deployment to Saudi Arabia, however, had obviously put those orders on hold. But as the air war began to wind down, Tonic Thiel allowed Tollini an early release for his new assignment.

"I had mixed feelings," he said. He wanted to get home to his wife and baby daughter; and he was eager to return to Okinawa, where he had spent his formative years as a green fighter pilot. "But I felt like this [the 58th Fighter Squadron] was 'my' squadron. These were 'my' guys, whom I had trained and watched over for the last year. I was extremely proud of them for everything they did and how well they did it. With few exceptions, everybody was willing to fly whatever was asked, regardless of how tired they were, or what the mission was."

Toward the end of February, Rick Tollini caught a flight to Ramstein Air Base, Germany, en route to Eglin. "Even though the war officially ended a couple of days after I got back to Eglin," he said, "the 58th got stuck waiting their turn for the massive exodus of troops and equipment that took more than four months to send over there." Six weeks after his arrival at Eglin, Tollini and his family packed their household goods and sailed across the Pacific to Okinawa.

But Rick Tollini wasn't the only member of the 58th to receive an early exodus from Desert Storm. In early February, Chief Matos received word that his brother had tragically passed away. The squadron leadership essentially told Matos: "Go home to Puerto Rico, bury your brother, and take your time coming back to Eglin." Before he left Tabuk, however, his superiors recommended him for the Bronze Star, in recognition of his adaptive, innovative leadership and his tireless efforts to keep the squadron at the highest readiness rates it had ever known. He thus turned over control of the maintenance section to another chief master sergeant, co-opted by the technical expertise of Todd McGirr.

Chapter 6
VICTORY

As the air war lumbered into its second month, coalition ground forces prepared for their initial assault into Iraq. On the evening of February 21, 1991, President Bush issued his final ultimatum: Saddam Hussein had twenty-four hours to withdraw from Kuwait or face destruction at the hands of coalition forces. Despite this ultimatum, however, the Iraqi dictator dug in his heels and told his troops to prepare for combat. From these developments, one thing was certain: the anticipated "Mother of All Battles" was coming to pass.

On February 24, the coalition ground forces began their initial push into Iraq. Although defense analysts and the normal variety of "experts" had anticipated several thousand Allied casualties, they were surprised to see Iraqi units (even the vaunted Republican Guard) being outclassed, outgunned, and outmaneuvered by American forces. But as American armored units rode forward, they suddenly found themselves under a curious downpour—black, greasy, rain. As it turned out, the Iraqi Army had resorted to its own cruel version of a "scorched earth" policy. In the wake of their retreat, they had set fire to Kuwait's oil fields, hoping to disrupt the advancing coalition. The smoke from these oil fires had drifted northward and had begun showering frontline forces with droplets of crude.

The 58th Fighter Squadron, meanwhile, continued flying escort missions and ground interdictions. By now most of the IQAF was in ruins. The pride of Saddam's air fleet had either been blown out of the sky, destroyed on the ground, or fled to Iran.

By mid-February, most pilots admitted to being bored.

As JB Kelk recalled, their most memorable sorties during the ground war consisted of spotting troops and vehicles... and then calling the AWACS to vector any nearby A-10s for a ground strafing. By this point in the war, the AWACS were letting the A-10s, F-15Es, and F-16s take most of the ground targets. "We kept doing our routine missions," Kelk continued, "but there wasn't any flying on the Iraqis' part."

The night of February 26, however, proved to be the last hurrah for the Allied air campaign. That night, coalition air squadrons pummeled Iraqi ground forces along Highway 80—the infamous "Highway of Death." In their desperate retreat from the Allied advance, the Iraqi Army had commandeered thousands of civilian vehicles (including buses, utility trucks, and private automobiles) to escape the onslaught of the US military.

Coalition air forces, however, were determined not to let them get away.

Throughout the night of February 26-27, scores of US Navy, Air Force, and Marine attack squadrons strafed the Iraqi columns as they tried to escape into the night. By sunrise, all that remained were several thousand charred automobile frames and many more dead Iraqis. When American ground forces passed through the Highway of Death, it was almost surreal. Using the front ends of their tanks, they had to push several of the abandoned Kuwaiti vehicles to the side of the road. Inside many of these commandeered vehicles, the charred remains of their Iraqi drivers gave mute evidence of the bombing campaign. These gruesome corpses appeared frozen in time, their hands still affixed to the steering wheels of the vehicles they had stolen. Although the 58th Fighter Squadron played no role in the Highway of Death, they were nonetheless astounded by the results. The fire, fury, and lethality of American air power had been put on full display.

Finally, on February 28, President Bush announced a cease-fire to the ground war. Barely 100 hours after the start of the Allied invasion, the Iraqis were in full retreat and Saddam was desperate to sue for peace. The "Mother of All Battles" had ended, and it was the Iraqi Army that had been destroyed. In their disastrous retreat, the Iraqis had fled Kuwait, leaving a devastated country in their wake. The fires from the oil fields were still burning out of control and much of Kuwait's antebellum wealth had been plundered. It would take a massive reconstruction effort to get the emirate back on its feet; but for now, the savagery of Iraq's occupation had ended. On March 3, 1991, General H. Norman Schwarzkopf, commander of UN Forces, met with several Iraqi generals in Safwan to discuss the terms of surrender.

While negotiations were ongoing, however, Mark Arriola and JB Kelk recalled the most unusual air tasking they had yet received: supersonic, low-level flights over Baghdad. "These were supposed to put the fear of God into the Iraqis and remind them that we were still there," said Mark. But the risk-to-reward ratio was so small, that none of the pilots appreciated the mission. For even at supersonic speeds, the F-15 was not invulnerable to SAM fire when flying at lower altitudes. Fortunately, wiser heads prevailed and CENTAF discontinued the low-level buzzing missions.

The IQAF, meanwhile, lay in shambles. They had lost more than 250 aircraft in the air and on the ground. By contrast, the IQAF confirmed only four air-to-air victories of its own. The Iraqi jets that had fled to Iran were impounded by the Ayatollah's government. Most of these newfound Iraqi airframes were impressed into Iranian service, with the Ayatollah claiming them as "reparations" for the Iran-Iraq War. The Iranians did, however, eventually return a handful of Sukhoi Su-25 attack planes.

Now that the war was officially over, the 58th was elated at the prospect of going home. After all, the cease-fire was still in effect and Saddam's war machine had been trounced after a 100-hour ground war. The 58th thought they'd remain at Tabuk for only a short while before flying back to Eglin.

Sadly, it was not to be.

Instead, as Saddam dragged his feet on signing the permanent cease-fire accord, US ground forces stationed themselves along the UN demarcation line (near An-Nasiriyah) to pressure the Iraqi government into signing.

Almost simultaneously, the United States realized that a military presence would still be necessary in the Persian Gulf. A Shi'ite rebellion had erupted during the postwar chaos while the Iraqi Kurds (already a targeted minority under the Ba'athist regime) attempted to flee the heavy-handed rule of Saddam Hussein. Thus, to protect the ethnic Kurds in the north, and the Shi'ite Muslims in the south, the US created and enforced the "No-Fly Zones" over northern and southern Iraq. Citing UN Resolution 688, the United States mandated that no Iraqi fixed-wing aircraft could enter the No-Fly Zones—else, they would be engaged by hostile fire.

The first aerial patrols over the No-Fly Zone were dubbed "Operation Provide Comfort." During that time (March - July 1991), American F-15 squadrons flew an assortment of combat air patrols and long-range reconnaissance missions.

And the 58th Fighter Squadron was among the first to take part.

"Because of the No-Fly Zones, our ROE [Rules of Engagement] changed," said Mark Arriola. "We couldn't employ any ordnance beyond visual range. We had to wait for positive ID [AWACS or VID] before we could shoot." Although the Iraqis were forbidden to launch any fixed-wing aircraft, they were, however, allowed to send helicopters into the air.

"I remember one time," Arriola continued, "Chuck and I ran an intercept on a Hind helicopter that was doing a resupply mission…and we did not get clearance to fire on that. They [CENTAF] were starting to allow the Iraqis an opportunity to mobilize internally to support any humanitarian efforts that may have been needed." But in the Ba'athist regime, "humanitarian efforts" were an unknown concept.

"Letting the Iraqis fly their helicopters wasn't the best idea," said JB Kelk. With the Shi'ite and Kurdish rebellions in full effect, it appeared that a regime change may have been on the horizon. "But the problem," Kelk continued, "is when you let the Iraqi Air Force fly very capable Soviet attack helicopters, they can suppress an uprising quite handily. There were no rules of engagement to engage helicopters, and it turned out that the Iraqis were using them against the Shi'ites."

"As soon as a cease fire was called," said Bill Thiel, "we started planning for redeployment. We wanted to get the hell out of there." CENTAF announced that all units would redeploy in the reverse order in which they came—"first in; first out"—as Thiel described it. "The people who been there the longest would be the first ones to come home." In reality, however, the US wanted to keep a residual force of fighter pilots in the area just in case the IQAF started generating more sorties. "Although by that time," Thiel added, "I don't think Saddam even had that capability." Still, the 58th Fighter Squadron was tasked to remain in theater throughout March 1991.

"And we were flying sorties right up until the day before we left," Thiel continued. These uneventful CAPs, however, were beginning to take their toll on the pilots, all of whom were eager to get home. After all, the IQAF had been defeated…and helicopter sightings were growing fewer and farther between. "We were just burning holes in the sky," said one pilot.

But the waiting came to an abrupt end on April 10, 1991.

That morning, Tonic Theil confirmed that the squadron would redeploy the following day, with an expected arrival at Eglin on April 12. "For redeployment," Thiel said, "we kind of spread the wealth around"—giving his airmen different options of departure times and layovers. For example, if a pilot had flown his F-15 on the transatlantic flight to Tabuk, he was given the option of returning home in the same F-15, or returning home on a commercial flight. If he chose the latter, another pilot who had flown to Tabuk aboard a transport would be given the opportunity to fly back in an F-15. As it turned out, there were several bachelor pilots who had flown to the gulf in their F-15s, and they were in no hurry to get back home. They instead took Thiel's offer to fly back commercially, "with some vacation time in Europe."

For Mark Arriola, however, the redeployment offered him a chance to cut loose and shake off any pretenses of Third World diplomacy. "Being a second lieutenant," he said, "you get stuck with all the sh*t jobs." But Tonic Thiel was about to give Mark the most unusual, and surprisingly entertaining, task of his young career.

"Nips," said Thiel, "I know there's a lot of pornography in the compound...I want it all disposed of."

True, despite the theater-wide mandate to burn or otherwise destroy their peepshow magazines, many servicemen had quietly retained theirs. And now Mark Arriola had the strange task of going door-to-door throughout the billets, collecting porn stashes for disposal. "I got these helmet bags from the life support shop, and I'm just going door-to-door like it's Halloween. I ended up collecting five helmet bags full of pornography! And now I'm thinking: 'All right dude, *what* am I going to do with five helmet bags of pornography?'"

He hadn't yet considered how he would dispose of it.

As he was getting his F-15 ready for departure, however, his crew chief had an idea: "If both of us could get up on this jet, we can lift the speed brake up just enough to where we can slide these things underneath that speed brake."

"That's brilliant!" Mark beamed.

"So, we throw these helmet bags on top of the jet...and we're able to slide them underneath that speed brake."

As Mark Arriola went airborne on the morning of April 11, he quickly vectored towards the nearest airbase in western Iraq. "And we get over top of this airfield at about 15,000 feet...I roll inverted, pop the speed brake open, and—*whoosh*—all this pornography starts flying to the ground in western Iraq," he chuckled. "I'm thinking to myself that there's some young Iraqi soldier sitting down there, and then all of a sudden, this porn falls right into his lap!"

Meanwhile, Tony "ET" Murphy and Cesar "Rico" Rodriguez were eager to get back home. Both men had left behind young families—Tony's wife Christine; Cesar's wife Trish, and the Rodriguez's young daughters. "We were one of the first units deployed, so we were pretty upset about returning so late," said ET Murphy.

Christine concurred: "It began to feel like their deployment would continue forever and we wouldn't get back to a normal life. We went on another roller coaster where the return dates changed as quickly as they were set. We became numb and didn't believe anything. When it was announced that they would come home on April 12, I thought: 'Yeah right, I'll wait until April 12 and, when I'm driving to the squadron to pick him up, I'll believe Tony's really coming home.'"

On the first leg of their flight back to Eglin, the squadron stopped in Zaragoza, Spain for a daylong layover. Of late, the Zaragoza Air Base had become a regular refuel point for planes travelling in and out of theater. It was also one of the emergency landing sites for NASA's Space Shuttle. "I'll never forget when we landed at Zaragoza," said Chuck Magill. "This American civilian contractor walks up to us and says: 'Gentlemen, this Bud's for you.' Then they open this airplane hangar…and it was filled with jukeboxes, pool tables, foosball tables, and more Anheuser-Busch products than I knew what to do with! The walls were just lined with cases and kegs."

But Bill Thiel had made it clear: "Limit yourselves to only one beer!"

Indeed, they would all be flying again in about 18 hours… not enough time to shake off the effects of a potential hangover.

Still, Zaragoza was a welcomed change of scenery. The whole country was abuzz preparing for the 1992 Olympics in Barcelona. "Oh man, just seeing green was neat," said ET Murphy. After months of flying above the monochromatic deserts of Iraq, the sudden infusion of springtime colors was nearly overwhelming. As he enjoyed the beer, chips, and salsa at the base, he reflected on how great it was to enjoy these simple fares. It had been a slice of Americana he had truly missed. "It was an incredible high to have a beer and be out of that country [Saudi Arabia]."

When the F-15s touched down at Eglin, they landed in four different flights of six airplanes, each spaced about thirty minutes apart. When Craig Underhill landed and taxied to the flight line, he was quickly greeted by Dave "Logger" Rose, who climbed the cockpit ladder to offer him a shot of Jeremiah Weed whiskey—the brand of choice among fighter pilots. These homecoming drinks were among the biggest reminders to Rose and Underhill that they were back in America. For many of these pilots, Zaragoza and Eglin had been their first opportunity in several months to enjoy a drink.

The bigger prize, however, was waiting just beyond the flight line. Roaring crowds of wives, family members, and local supporters were gathered to give the 58th Fighter Squadron a heroes' welcome. Among them was Jose Matos, who had just returned from his brother's funeral in Puerto Rico. True to his sense of duty, Matos went out to the flight line and helped the Wing Commander, Colonel Parsons, out of his cockpit. The immediate post-flight maintenance, however, could wait...because now was a time for celebration.

"Homecoming was huge," recalled Bill Thiel. The families of the 58th, along with the rest of the 33d Fighter Wing had come out to see them. Another surprise visitor was General John Loh, the commander-in-chief of US Tactical Air Command, the command group responsible for all fighter formations in the Air Force. "I think that it [Loh's visit] was largely because we had been so successful," Thiel surmised. "We were the top-killing squadron in theater: 16 aerial victories without losing a single friendly aircraft." A while later, the squadron would also receive a visit from Vice President Dan Quayle, offering his personal congratulations and well wishes.

As the exuberant families met their pilots on the flight line, the throng of reunited loved ones gathered into the squadron bar for an hour-long celebration. "I dropped into McDonalds on the way home to get a whole bunch of stuff," said Murphy, "but my stomach was so small from not eating that I couldn't even finish a Big Mac and fries." As he returned home with Christine, he realized just how much his sleep patterns had been disrupted by war. Indeed, he woke up at 3:00 AM just to make nachos. "Man, that was great!" he beamed. "It was wonderful to open up a refrigerator and have a choice." Still, for many pilots in the 58th, today's homecoming had been a bittersweet moment— their warm welcome was a far cry from what their forefathers had experienced during Vietnam.

After returning from the Gulf, the squadron gave every airman a two-week furlough to decompress from the war and spend time with family. For the married pilots like Cesar Rodriguez and Tony Murphy, it was a welcomed opportunity to pick up where they had left off. For the single pilots and crewmen, however, the time was ripe to sow their wild oats. Nightlife in the Florida Panhandle hadn't slowed down, and the local ladies were ablaze with intrigue at the victorious fighter jocks who had just returned from Iraq.

Soon, however, it was back to "business as usual." As all the planes, pilots, and maintenance assets were accounted for, the squadron began flying more practice maneuvers in preparation for the next rounds of Red Flag and William Tell. With their skills sharpened by war, however, these mock dogfights and aerial gunnery contests seemed stale by comparison.

In the skies over Iraq, the 58th Fighter Squadron had emerged victorious in combat against a numerically-superior enemy. Their victory against the IQAF had been a nod to the old adage: "The more you sweat in peace, the less you bleed in combat." In the final analysis, however, the factors that contributed to the squadron's victory were both technological *and* metaphysical. The IQAF may have been the "best and brightest" of Saddam's forces, but their training, maintenance, and overall airmanship paled in comparison to the US Air Force and its western allies. The F-15 was technologically-superior to the MiG-29 and many of its counterparts. But the qualitative differences among the F-15, MiG-29, MiG-23, and Mirage F1 were only part of the equation. The deciding factor lay in the human realm: better training and better tactics had paved the way for the squadron's victory over the IQAF.

Over the past two years, the 58th Fighter Squadron had seen a world transformed. After years of studying tactics and equipment of the Eastern Bloc air forces, they saw the Cold War end right before their eyes. Cyclic aerial patrols along the Iron Curtain (and fleeting encounters with Soviet MiGs) had ended without a shot being fired. As the military drew down its Cold War stance, it rose to fight a Middle Eastern dictator who commanded the largest air force in the region. While the Iraqis had strength in numbers, their equipment and skills couldn't keep pace with the US military and its coalition partners.

"It was a high time for the nation," said JB Kelk, "in the sense that we had just come off the downers in Vietnam and the Iran rescue mission. Now, we had this massive military buildup...frankly to outspend the Russians and win the Cold War, which we did. And then we put that training to use, not to defeat the Russians, but the Iraqis."

In the 58th Fighter Squadron, airmen from every walk of life had come together to serve their country. Unlike many of their forefathers, these pilots and crewmen had joined voluntarily. Some had joined for the adventure; some had joined for the romance of flight; while others had joined as a means of upward mobility. Whatever their reasons, they all came with a sense of duty and love of country. These young men demonstrated the vitality and professionalism of America's post-Vietnam Air Force. Collectively, they showed what any unit can accomplish when it has realistic training, individual initiative, good leadership, and pride in the mission. Although the men of the 58th Fighter Squadron went their separate ways after 1991, their legacy lives on as the top "MiG Killers" of Operation Desert Storm.

Epilogue:
AFTER THE STORM

At this writing, none of the Desert Storm veterans from the 58th Fighter Squadron remain on active duty. Of the junior pilots, Cesar "Rico" Rodriguez and Jon "JB" Kelk stayed in uniform the longest. When Rodriguez redeployed from the Gulf, he was reassigned to the 9th Air Force at Shaw AFB, South Carolina, where he served as Chief of the Air-to-Air Branch until August 1994. Upon graduating from the Air Command and Staff College in 1995, he reported to Ramstein Air Base, Germany, serving two years at Headquarters Allied Air Forces Central Europe. In October 1997, however, he returned to the job he loved the most—flying the F-15 Eagle. New orders assigned him to the 493d Fighter Squadron at RAF Lakenheath, England.

By now a lieutenant colonel, Rodriguez deployed with the 493d in support of Operation Allied Force—the air war over Kosovo. NATO, already having a foothold in the region due to its peacekeeping missions in Bosnia, was determined to drive the Yugoslavs from Kosovo on the grounds of humanitarian intervention. To affect these goals, American F-15s once again returned to the fray.

While the F-15E Strike Eagles pounded Serbian targets from the air, the F-15C resumed its role as the king of aerial combat. During Allied Force, the Federal Republic of Yugoslavia Air Force sent its ailing fleet of MiG-29s to intercept NATO aircraft operating within Yugoslav airspace. By 1999, however, there was little that this fleet could actually accomplish.

Following the breakup of the original Yugoslavia, the national air force had shrunk to one-third of its former size. Subsequent to the Dayton Peace Accords in 1995, the Yugoslav Air Force reduced its numbers even further. Thus, by the time Allied Force began, they had barely sixty MiG-21s and sixteen MiG-29s. Even before the war, the Yugoslav government had been struggling to keep its fleet of MiG-29s operational. Therefore, it seemed inevitable that these ailing MiGs would meet their demise against the incoming F-15s.

On March 24, 1999, Cesar Rodriguez would meet the third MiG-29 of his career over the city of Pristina. "There were two missions on this first night," said Rodriguez, "both spearheaded by F-15s of the 493d Fighter Squadron." The targets for this mission were primarily in Montenegro—radar and air defense sites positioned to deny access to Pristina. "The strike was designed to break a hole in this SAM belt, and to open access for the CAS [Close Air Support] assets that needed to get into Kosovo from the west."

That night, Rodriguez flew as part of a four-ship flight. His wingman was Lieutenant William "Wild Bill" Denim, one of the youngest pilots in the squadron. Denim had just completed his "check rides" and, thus far, had logged less than 100 hours of flight time in the F-15. "In fact," Rodriguez said, "he would finish the war with more combat time than peacetime flying in the F-15."

Heading north towards Montenegro, Rodriguez and his wingman found an initial radar contact 25 miles from a templated airfield. At first, it appeared to be an enemy air patrol, but its orbiting flight pattern and slow airspeed suggested that it wasn't a fighter patrol. While the flight leader focused on this enemy flight group, Rodriguez and Denim maintained their focus on Pristina. "Our main task was to ensure that nothing took off from Pristina heading towards Montenegro that might intercept our strike."

Suddenly, from a distance of 70 miles, Rodriguez got radar contact of a fast mover climbing to 10,000 feet. With his onboard instrumentation, Rodriguez confirmed that this lurking bandit was a MiG-29. "I directed my element to start a climb, jettison tanks, and push it up. This would give our [missiles] greater range and since we were on the front edge of the strike package, I wanted to shoot as soon as possible...start the shooting match on our terms, not the MiG's."

Closing within 20 miles, Rodriguez fired an AIM-120 missile. Rodriguez hadn't realized it, but he had accelerated to Mach 1.3. Thus, as the missile glided off his wing, it appeared as though the AIM-120 was flying alongside him. "The missile took a couple of seconds to build up momentum and accelerate out in front of me, and during that time, I thought I might have had a bad missile." As the missile plowed forward into the night, Rodriguez could see the faint glow of the MiG-29's engine—"about the size of a dime," he recalled.

As he looked through his sights, he lost visual contact of the MiG, as it was dark outside. "But I was counting down the seconds left for the missile to impact." As the counter reached zero, a huge fireball erupted. "Because the western mountains were still covered in snow," he continued, "the fireball literally lit up the sky as it reflected off the snow-covered mountains. The only thing I had ever seen like this was when they turn on all the lights at an NFL stadium, except this was like five times that bright; it really lit up the whole sky. In fact, an F-15E WSO about 85 miles to the southwest of my fireball, heard my 'Splash' call and simultaneously saw the bright glow. He became suspicious of what might have detonated up there, since the glow was so bright! As it turned out, it was just that MiG-29 exploding."

Reflecting on his mission in the Balkans, Rodriguez said: "Operation Allied Force represented a turning point in the understanding of warfare by the average fighter pilot. As one of a few Desert Storm veterans in our squadron, I kind of felt it was my responsibility to help guys understand their role in actual combat, and the impact of combat on our squadron...and our families back home. I also made a point to help the young guys understand the political ramifications of being armed with an air-to-air machine, and that you are sending a political statement any time you hit that pickle button.

"Allied Force represented a political tightrope, where US forces and NATO forces were coming together for a political objective. We realized at that point that NATO had fallen behind in its training and technological investment. As a result, some of the tactics that were employed had to be 'watered down' significantly so that other partners could play completely in the entire operation. We also had a unique scenario where, as the US leadership from SHAPE [Supreme Headquarters, Allied Powers Europe] was directing airpower, they were not always airmen, and hence sometimes that direction was poor. It was common to go after targets that had already been struck, or going after targets that had no impact on forcing Yugoslavia to surrender."

Rodriguez concluded: "I say it was a turning point because, unlike Desert Storm, where we had no idea what was going on, we were just the execution element, we were actively involved in planning the air campaign over

Yugoslavia. Unfortunately, when these recommendations got to SHAPE, they were often changed, and airmen were put into harm's way striking targets that had no significance. But that's a whole other aspect of this battle space. The actions of the 493d were significant in developing tactics for both day and night employment that are still used by the F-15 community." With three confirmed aerial victories (two MiG-29s and a MiG-23), Cesar Rodriguez has achieved more air-to-air kills than any American pilot since Vietnam.

Following Kosovo, Rodriguez returned stateside for another staff assignment, this time as the Assistant Chief of Flight Safety with Air Combat Command at Langley AFB. In August 2001, he reported to the Naval War College (NWC) where he received a Master's degree in Strategic Studies. Following his graduation from NWC, he reported to the 366th Fighter Wing at Mountain Home AFB, Idaho. During this time, Rodriguez returned to Iraq and Kuwait as Commander of the 332nd Expeditionary Operations Group (332nd Air Expeditionary Wing). His return to the Gulf was unique because it overlapped the end of Operation Southern Watch (over the Southern "No-Fly Zone") and the start of Operation Iraqi Freedom. Returning from the Gulf in Spring 2004, he assumed command of the 355th Mission Support Group at Davis-Monthan AFB, Arizona, as his final assignment. He retired in November 2006. Today, he resides in Arizona, where he is a top-level executive for Raytheon Missiles & Defense.

After Desert Storm, Jon "JB" Kelk transitioned into the Air National Guard. He enjoyed being a fighter pilot but, amidst the postwar downsizing, he knew the military was no longer a growth industry. "If I learned anything from my Vietnam flight magazines," he said, "it's that when you downsize the Air Force, fewer cockpits mean fewer jobs." The Air National Guard, however, was always on the lookout for transitioning pilots, and offered great incentives for continued service.

"While I was in the Gulf War," he said, "the St. Louis squadron was converting to F-15s from F-4s. And a lot of guys I knew and respected were in that unit. So, while I was over in the desert, I sent them a note and they held my application. When I came back, I went out to interview in St. Louis and they hired me." Being in the Air National Guard, as he recalled, was a "good fit," because it allowed him to focus almost exclusively on flying as opposed to the staff jobs that often befell active duty pilots. Moreover, it allowed him to continue serving while pursuing a career in commercial aviation; he was hired by American Airlines the following year. Kelk served with the St. Louis Squadron from 1992 until its deactivation in 2009. During that time, the Air National Guard went from being a "strategic reserve" to an "operational reserve." Indeed, as deployments to the Middle East increased throughout the 1990s, the Air National Guard took a significant load of the operational tasks "to keep the active duty Air Force from burning out."

When the St. Louis squadron stood down, JB Kelk (now a Brigadier General) began looking for another job in another state's Air Guard. Luckily, California was looking for a new Air National Guard Commander—someone to be in charge of the state's air forces. Kelk accepted the job concurrent with a two-star promotion. "I commanded the Air Guard in California for five years," he said, "which was a really interesting job; I learned a lot about the state and new missions in the Air Force I wasn't previously aware of."

In his final assignment, he was the Air National Guard Assistant to the Commander of United States Air Forces Europe/Africa—the command group responsible for air and space operations throughout Europe, Africa, and parts of Eurasia. "That was a great gig for me, he said, because I was back in Europe," where he had spent many of his formative years as a fighter pilot. "It was neat to go back and see Europe without all the borders. Back in the eighties, even traveling around Western Europe, you needed a passport to get between the various countries. Now you can travel freely throughout Europe, including all the places we used to train against. So, it was really neat traveling to the former Soviet bloc countries...Estonia, Poland, Slovakia, Romania...that was a really nice way to finish out a career." Jon Kelk retired from the Air National Guard in 2019, completing 38 years of total service. Today, he still flies for American Airlines, conducting check rides and simulator exercises for new pilots and rising captains.

Rick "Kluso" Tollini returned to the 12th Fighter Squadron in Okinawa, where he served as the Squadron Weapons Officer from 1991-94. In this capacity, he led the development of the squadron's AIM-120 Advanced Medium-Range Air-to-Air (AMRAAM) missile tactics, "as we were the first fully-operational squadron with the AIM-120," he said. At the time, the AMRAAM missile was being touted as the next-generation BVR projectile, capable of all-weather day-and-night operations. With its combined upgrades, the AMRAAM had the advantage of being a "fire-and-forget" weapon system—meaning that the pilot did not have to track it as he would the AIM-7 Sparrow. The problem, however, was that the AIM-120 was still having developmental issues.

"The AIM-120," said Tollini, "was actually first fielded, probably ill-advisedly, near the end of Desert Storm. I think it was more of a ploy to try to get the military's newest 'toy' some exposure to combat and maybe even to shoot down an enemy aircraft." The pilots, however, discovered that the F-15's AMRAAM software had enough glitches to render the missile inoperable. "The other issue," said Tollini, "was that this was an entirely new generation of AAMs, and it can take months or even years of extensive training and experience to understand how to best utilize and integrate new technology. You don't really want to do that in the middle of a shooting war, unless there is some extreme need to do so, and our AIM-7M missiles had been doing their job just fine in most cases." Thus, his job at Kadena was to "help create a level of operational expertise and viable tactics for use of the new AMRAAM."

Returning stateside in 1994 to attend the Air Command and Staff College, Tollini then reported to the Pacific Air Force (PACAF) Headquarters at Hickam AFB, Hawaii. Becoming PACAF's Chief of Special Programs/Air Combat Requirements, Tollini led the team in developing several upgrades to the F-15C. These included the new Pratt & Whitney 220 engine, AESA radar, and numerous avionics software updates. "I was also able to gain access to future programs and help shape forthcoming missile and advanced fighter programs like the F-22."

But, as with any job, there were drawbacks and frustrations, "and most of those," he said, "involved decisions on procurement programs emanating from the highest levels of the Air Force and our government." Perhaps the biggest mistake Tollini witnessed was the hasty decision to procure more than 700 F-22 Raptors to replace the F-15C. As a result, many of the F-15's critical upgrades lost funding. As Tollini explained it, the F-15C upgrades "would compete directly against the Air Force's prized F-22 program and the 700-plus airframe buy." He postulated that a better option would have been to cut the F-22 procurement in half—"to about 350, which was a number that Congress had already offered to the Air Force"—and divert the savings into the F-15 programs. This, in turn, would give the Air Force "two very complimentary and impressive airframes for the air superiority mission for the next 30-plus years." In the end, however, Rick Tollini shook his head in frustration as the Air Force went forward with the 750-Raptor plan...and ended up with less than a quarter of its desired airframes—187

Raptors in total. To make matters worse, the F-22 would not become operational for the next several years. Meanwhile, the Air Force realized that the F-15 was still a vital airframe, but now its critical upgrades had gone unfunded.

In 1998, Rick Tollini returned to Okinawa for his final tour with the 12th Fighter Squadron. "I was the Operations Officer until the squadron stood down in 1999." By now a lieutenant colonel, Tollini stayed in Okinawa and assumed command of the 18th Operational Support Squadron (OSS). By this time, however, Rick and his family had begun contemplating retirement. "I had achieved so much in the previous 18–19 years in the Air Force," he said. "I had grown as a fighter pilot and as a leader, but the one thing I could not quantify was if I had grown at all as a human being." As he recalled, the world of a fighter pilot was very small. And the fighter community was often insulated from the rest of the Air Force. This culture had made the fighter community unique, but as Rick conceded: "It does not allow much of a vector for personal growth." In that regard, the OSS command allowed him to reconnect with people and missions beyond the flying force. In his final assignment, Tollini worked for a year and a half in the Air Force Inspector General Office at Kadena Air Base. He retired in 2003.

Since his retirement, however, he has had a colorful and rewarding civilian career. Today, he works as a contract instructor pilot at the F-15C Mission Training Center at Kadena. In his off-hours, he is a professional musician and recording artist. Combining elements of folk and rock music, Rick Tollini performs under the stage name "Kluso" and has played at numerous venues in Japan and the United States. His songs and albums are available on iTunes. Rick Tollini recently published his own memoirs, Call Sign Kluso, which tells the remarkable story of his life and career before, during, and after Desert Storm.

Chuck "Sly" Magill returned to the Marine Corps as a celebrated hero. He was the only Marine aviator in Desert Storm to achieve an aerial kill. And his accomplishment was all the more intriguing because he had done it while flying an Air Force jet. Having made history and having gained extensive knowledge on Air Force interoperability, Magill became a highly in-demand speaker at various air installations, including the Navy Fighter Weapons School ("Top Gun") and the Marine Corps Weapons & Tactics Instructor Course.

Having a family, however, quickly changed his outlook on the prospect of continuing his service. "In the Marine Corps, we deploy all the time," he said. "Back in the eighties, in the Air Force, you'd generally go over to Kadena or Bitburg, and then come back. But in the Navy or Marine Corps, you're on a boat and you're deployed a lot." In fact, Magill deployed to Desert Shield while his wife, Lisa, was five months pregnant. Their daughter Caitlin was born on January 18, 1991, just as he was returning from his second mission. When he redeployed to Eglin, he came home to his now four-month-old daughter.

It was then that Chuck Magill began to consider other career options.

"I never thought about doing anything other than flying fighters," he said, "and it was a really hard decision, but family is much more important." At the time, Magill had been selected for major, and was looking at an assignment as an Operations Officer aboard a marine carrier squadron—a billet that would almost guarantee a longer time away from his family. "So, I got out, got into the Reserves, and started flying airlines." Like many of the 58th alumni (including Mark Arriola, Bruce Till, Larry Pitts, and Dave Rose), Chuck Magill was hired by Southwest Airlines and eventually rose to become the Vice President of Flight Operations, where he served for many years. While building his career as a civilian pilot, he served an additional ten years in the Marine Corps Reserve. After years of flying for Southwest, Magill retired for good in 2016.

After Desert Storm, Mark "Nips" Arriola moved farther down the Florida Panhandle to Tyndall Air Force Base as an F-15 Instructor. He left the active Air Force in 1995 and transitioned into the Texas Air National Guard. While flying for Southwest Airlines, he joined the 147th Fighter-Interceptor Wing at Ellington Field in Houston, Texas. Although the 147th was an F-16 unit, Mark took readily to the lighter and leaner single-engine jet. "With the F-16s, we deployed to Central America and stayed at Howard Air Force Base in Panama. We did a bunch of counter-narcotics and drug interdiction stuff down there during the summers."

By 2001, he had transitioned into the Air Force Reserve and spent the next several years as an admissions counselor for his alma mater, the US Air Force Academy. He retired from the Air Force Reserve in 2016, culminating 28 years of combined service. Today, he continues to fly for Southwest Airlines.

Larry "Cherry" Pitts completed his time at Eglin with orders to the Air Command and Staff College at Maxwell AFB, Alabama. At some point during the 1990s, Pitts sustained a critical back injury that prohibited him from flying ejection seat-equipped aircraft. Barred from the fighter community due to medical reasons, Pitts was nonetheless happy to retain his flight status and he transitioned into the E-3 Sentry AWACS aircraft...the same "eyes in the sky" that had guided him onto several enemy MiGs over Iraq. He later served as an Operations Officer and Squadron Commander at Tinker AFB, Oklahoma before commanding the USAF Officer Training School. He retired as a full Colonel in 2004. Following his retirement, Larry served briefly as a corporate pilot before transitioning to Southwest Airlines.

Craig "Mole" Underhill left the 58th in December 1993. "I went to the Air Staff at Langley Air Force Base working for Air Combat Command [ACC]." Although not a flying position, it gave him two years of higher-echelon staff and planning experience. "I started off as the AMRAAM AIM-120 project officer which, at the time, was the number one program at ACC." He returned to flight status in 1996, flying F-15s for the 71st Fighter Squadron at Langley. "Then I went over to be Chief of Weapons for the 1st Fighter Wing, and later, the Chief of Standards & Evaluations."

Craig's next assignment took him across the country to Nellis Air Force Base, Nevada. As the site of the annual Red Flag exercises (and home to the renowned 57th Adversary Tactics Group), Nellis offered perhaps the greatest broadening opportunities for a mid-career fighter pilot. The home-stationed aggressor units regularly studied enemy tactics and employed them in training scenarios against lines squadrons every year. As the new Aggressor Operations Officer, Underhill described it as "one of the best jobs for a non-combat assignment," with the added benefit of keeping his flight hours current. "It was just a blast," he said. "When I was there, we had about 10-12 pilots assigned, and they were all instructor pilots…for the most part hand-picked. We also had five or six guys attached from the Thunderbirds [the Air Force's aerial demonstration team] who were waiting for their follow-on assignments. But what a great mission to teach other pilots how to get through air-to-air combat."

Reflecting on his experience from the aggressor side of Red Flag, Underhill noted that: "Red Flag was designed to get somebody through their first ten combat sorties." Indeed, during Vietnam and Korea, the Air Force discovered that if a pilot could survive his first ten sorties, he would likely survive the war. "So Red Flag was designed to put them in a combat situation where they could learn under the hardest conditions." Craig recalled a video clip of another pilot during Desert Storm who had just returned from his first strike mission. That pilot had said his mission was tough, "but I think my last Red Flag mission was harder."

Craig Underhill spent the remainder of his active duty career at Nellis. He commanded the 64th Aggressor Squadron, and later became the deputy commander for Red Flag. He retired in 2004 and currently flies for Southwest Airlines.

Tony "ET" Murphy returned to Elgin with an assignment for the 85th Test Squadron. After attending the USAF Fighter Weapons School, he served as an Instructor Pilot and Weapons Officer in the F-15 Formal Training Unit (FTU) at Tyndall AFB. Like most mid-level career officers, ET Murphy spent a few years on staff, most notably at the Pentagon. He returned to the 33d Fighter Wing a few years later as the Wing Weapons Officer before assuming command of the 85th Test Squadron (where he had initially served upon returning from Desert Storm). He later became the Deputy Group Commander of the Weapons Systems Evaluation Program (WSEP) at Tyndall AFB before his retirement. He and his wife, Christine, currently reside in Winchester, Tennessee.

Bill "Tonic" Thiel relinquished command of the 58th Fighter Squadron in November 1991. In recognition for his leadership during the Gulf War, he received an early promotion to full Colonel that same year. Reflecting on his time in the 58th, he said: "It was the best job I ever had in the Air Force."

After relinquishing command, Thiel became the Deputy Ops Group Commander at Eglin for nearly ten months before attending the National War College (NWC) at Fort

McNair in Washington, DC. NWC was considered the premier senior-service war college in the nation. Each branch of the service had its own war college, but NWC sought an equal enrollment of Army, Air Force, Navy, and Marine officers for attendance. Its goal was to teach senior military officers the complexities of strategic thinking within a joint-operations environment.

Graduating from NWC in June 1993, Thiel became the Support Group Commander at Griffiss Air Force Base. Although it was a non-flying job, there was no shortage of responsibility. "You're basically in charge of all non-flying operations," he said. "You own the BX [Base Exchange]; you own the communications squadron; you own the civil engineering squadron; you own the personnel squadron; you own the security police squadron...basically all the ground-pounders. These were a great group of folks. It was really an eye-opening assignment." However, by the time Thiel had accepted his new command, Griffiss Air Force Base had already been tapped for deactivation—another casualty of the post-Cold War downsizing. Thus, after only two years in command, Griffiss Air Force Base closed; and Thiel was reassigned to MacDill Air Force Base for another tour as Support Group Commander. Leading the support group from 1995-97, Thiel's career took an interesting turn when he was asked to organize a newly-activated air refueling wing at MacDill.

That fall, he finally returned to Eglin, hoping for another rated position aboard the F-15. Instead, he was named the Deputy Director of the Combat Identification and Evaluations Team. Years earlier, the Air Force had created this task force as a means of resolving the perennial misidentifications of friendly aircraft that had occurred during Desert Storm. Although it was a meaningful assignment, it took Thiel farther away from the flying positions he loved. In a way, his career path illustrated the fate that befell many a talented pilot—the more rank he achieved, the less flight time he had.

By the fall of 1998, as he became eligible for another transfer, the Air Force offered him another assignment as the Chief of Safety for the First Air Force. "If it was a flying job, I might have taken it." Instead, he opted to retire in December 1998. Unlike many of the squadron's alumni, Bill Thiel did not pursue a career in civil aviation. "I went to work for SAIC...and I became a division manager for them"—overseeing defense contracts for various Air Force applications. At one point, as a division manager, Thiel was responsible for more than $70 million in business programs. He retired for good in 2016 and currently lives in the Fort Walton Beach area.

Jose Matos became the Quality Assurance Manager for the 33d Fighter Wing after Desert Storm. The position placed him in charge of evaluating all 72 airplanes within the unit. "I did that for a year and a half," he said, "and from there, I went to Iceland"—as chief of the Aircraft Maintenance Unit (AMU) rendering support to the 57th Fighter-Interceptor Squadron at Keflavik Air Base. The 57th was one of several NATO air units assigned to the perennial Icelandic Air Policing mission. The mission itself was a relic from the Cold War era, providing Iceland with a rapid air defense capability against the Warsaw Pact. Even after the fall of the Soviet Union, the missions continued since Iceland had no standing army or air force. "I had my family with me," he continued, "and let me tell you, Iceland is the best place you can take your kids!"

After turning the Keflavik AMU into one of the top-performing units in NATO, the local wing commander invited Matos to be his top enlisted aide. "It was kind of like being a Command Sergeant Major in the Army," he recalled.

After a few years in Iceland, he returned stateside with orders to Pope Air Force Base, North Carolina. "I was going to retire to North Carolina," he said. "We had already bought a 12-acre parcel of land out there." Jose Matos retired in 1997, completing nearly 30 years of active service.

His final year in uniform, however, was tinged with sadness. On June 25, 1996, he awoke to the news of the Khobar Towers bombing in Saudi Arabia. At the time, the Khobar complex was housing UN coalition members assigned to Operation Southern Watch, the ongoing mission over the southern No-Fly Zone. These included members of the 33d Fighter Wing, including many of Chief Matos's closest friends. In fact, twelve of the nineteen airmen who perished in the attack were members of the 33d Fighter Wing, with an additional 105 personnel wounded. "Not a day goes by that I don't think about my friends in the Khobar Towers." In his later years, Chief Matos returned to his native Puerto Rico. After a long battle with cancer, Jose Matos tragically passed away on April 8, 2021.

BIBLIOGRAPHY

PRIMARY SOURCES

Interviews:

Interviews with Mark Arriola. July-August 2020.

Interviews with Rich Hardy. August-September 2020.

Interviews with Jon Kelk. December 2020.

Interviews with Chuck Magill. May-December 2020.

Interviews with Jose Matos. June-November 2020.

Interviews with Todd McGirr. August-September 2020.

Interviews with Larry Pitts. May-June 2020.

Interviews with Cesar Rodriguez. May-August 2020.

Interviews with Bill Thiel. August-November 2020.

Interviews with Bruce Till. May-August 2020.

Interviews with Rick Tollini. May-August 2020.

Interviews with Craig Underhill. May-August 2020.

Personal Papers:

The Personal Papers of Mark Arriola. Flight logs, various photographs, and maps pertaining to Desert Shield/Desert Storm.

Archival Material:

National Archives and Records Administration II. College Park, MD

Record Group 330. Records from the OSD, 1921-2008. Photographic Collection.

Published Works:

Brown, Craig. *Debrief: A Complete History of US Aerial Engagements, 1981-present.* Altgen: Schiffer Publishing, 2007.

Herlik, Ed. *Separated by War: An Oral History by Desert Storm Fliers and Their Families.* New York: McGraw-Hill, 1994.

Tollini, Rick. *Call Sign Kluso: An American Fighter Pilot in Mr. Reagan's Air Force.* Havertown: Casemate Publishers, 2021.

SECONDARY SOURCES

Atkinson, Rick. *Crusade: The Untold Story of the Persian Gulf War.* New York: Houghton Mifflin, 1993.

Davies, Steve. *F-15C Eagle Units in Combat.* Oxford: Osprey Publishing, 2005.

Davies, Steve. *F-15E Strike Eagle Units in Combat 1990–2005.* Oxford: Osprey Publishing, 2005.

Davies, Steve, and Doug Dildy. *F-15 Eagle Engaged: The World's Most Successful Jet Fighter.* Oxford: Osprey Publishing, 2007.

Drendel, Lou. *And Kill MiGs: Air-to-Air Combat from Vietnam to the Gulf War.* Norcross: Squadron/Signal Publications, 1997.

Hallion, Richard. *Storm Over Iraq: Air Power and the Gulf War.* New York: Smithsonian Institution, 2015.

Morse, Stan. *Gulf Air War Debrief.* London: Airtime Pub, 1991.

McCarthy, Donald J. *The Raptors: All F-15 and F-16 Aerial Combat Victories.* Altgen: Schiffer Publishing, 2017.

Printed in Great Britain
by Amazon

12867180R00133